HAPPY DAYS

Art Therapy Coloring Book

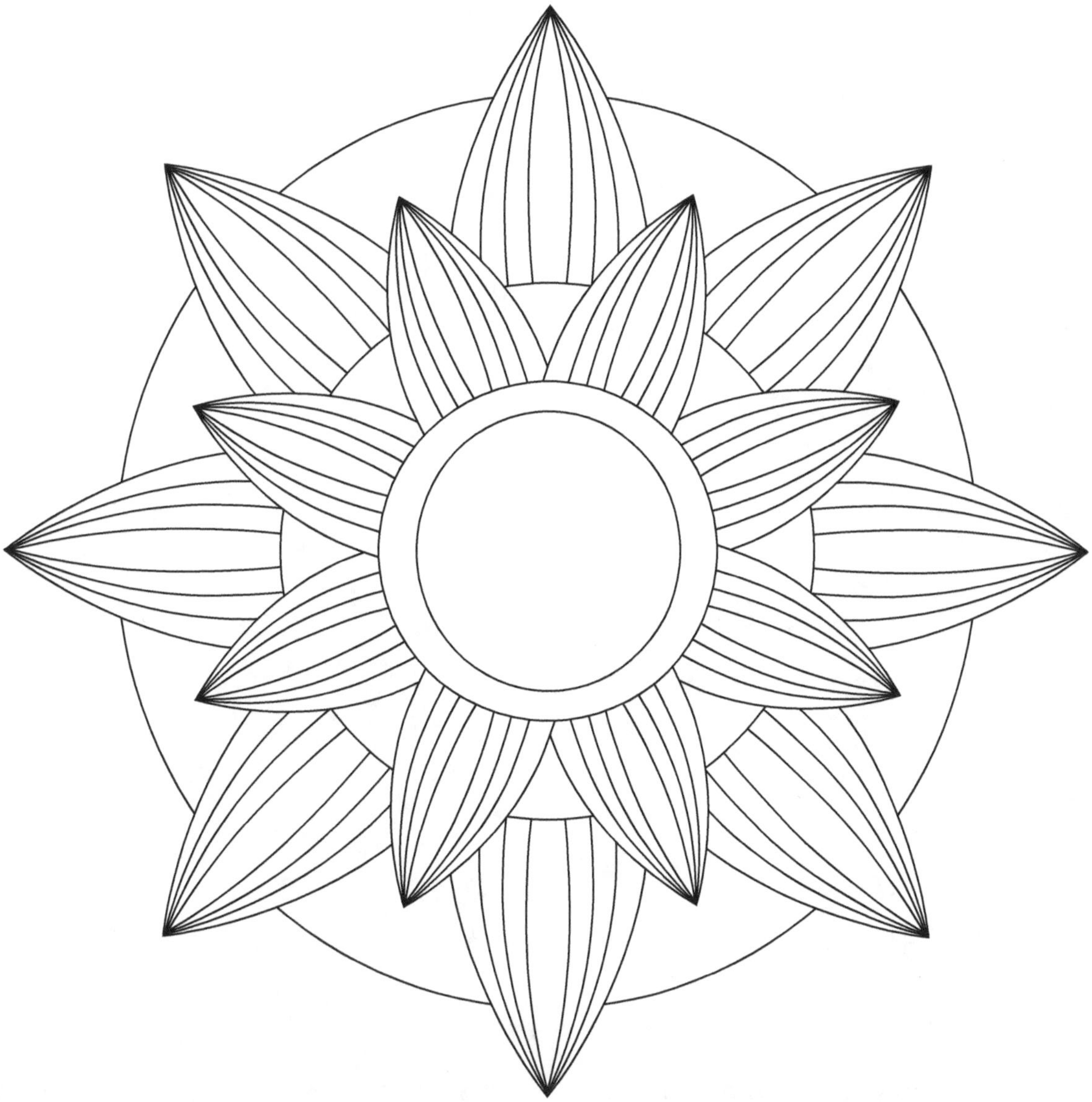

Tammy Groves Thornton

ISBN-13: 978-1523961412

ISBN-10: 1523961414

Welcome to the wonderful world of coloring!

Coloring is not just fun...it is calming, therapeutic and the perfect antidote to life's everyday stresses.

Using your imagination, my drawings, and whatever medium you want - crayons, markers, color pencils, pens, etc. - you can create a beautiful and unique new world of stillness and peace.

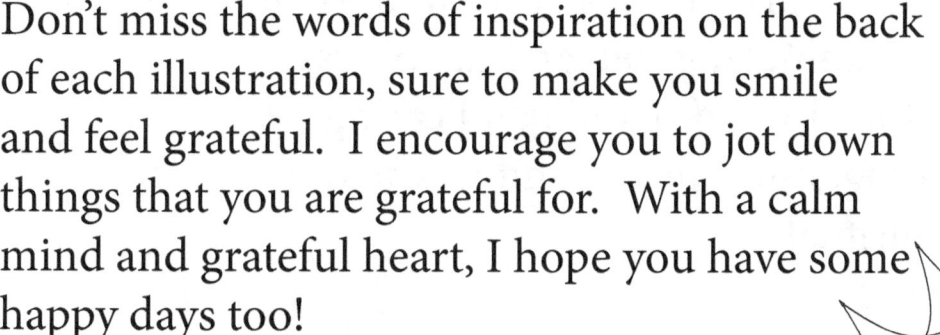

Happy Days contains more than 50 mandalas and intricate patterns just waiting to be filled with vibrant colors. It is designed to unlock your imagination and help you relax and express yourself.

Don't miss the words of inspiration on the back of each illustration, sure to make you smile and feel grateful. I encourage you to jot down things that you are grateful for. With a calm mind and grateful heart, I hope you have some happy days too!

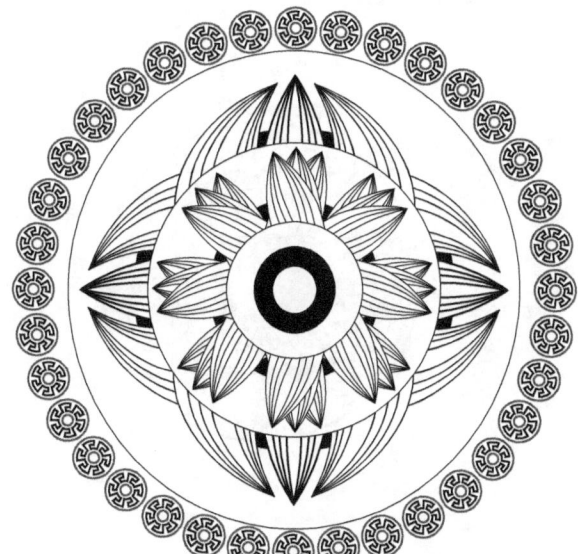

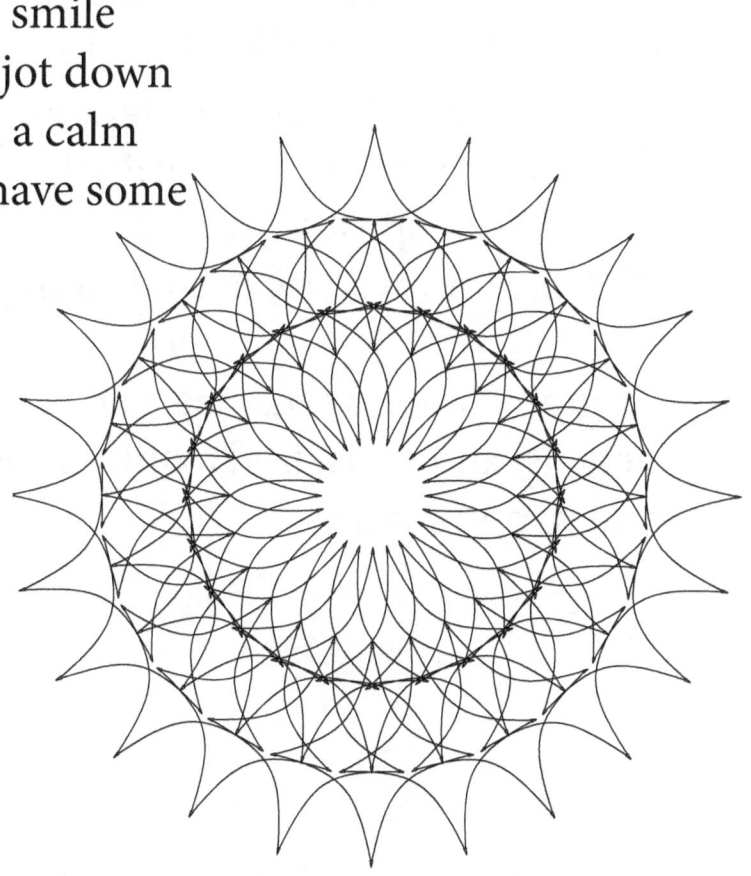

The word Mandala means "circle". A Mandala represents wholeness, the search for completeness, and self-unity. The mandala appears to us in all aspects of life, such as the Earth, the Sun, the Moon and more obviously the circles of life encompassing friends, family and communities. Mandalas are circular designs symbolizing the notion that life is never ending. Mandalas are used for meditation purposes allowing the individual meditating to become one with the universe.

When coloring your mandala, I encourage you to choose colors that appeal to you, colors that relax you, colors that calm you, or colors that make you happy. And if you can't decide, here are some suggestions to get you started:

RED for strength, high energy, and passion
PINK for love, intuition, and the feminine
ORANGE for creativity, transformation, self-awareness, and intuition
YELLOW for learning, wisdom, laughter, and happiness
GREEN for physical healing, love of nature, and caring
BLUE for emotional healing, inner peace, and meditation
PURPLE for all things spiritual
WHITE for spiritual focus
BLACK for mystery, deep thinking, and individuality

So grab your crayons, markers, color
pencils, and pens, find a quiet spot,
and happy coloring!!!

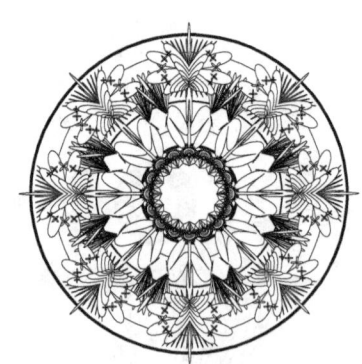

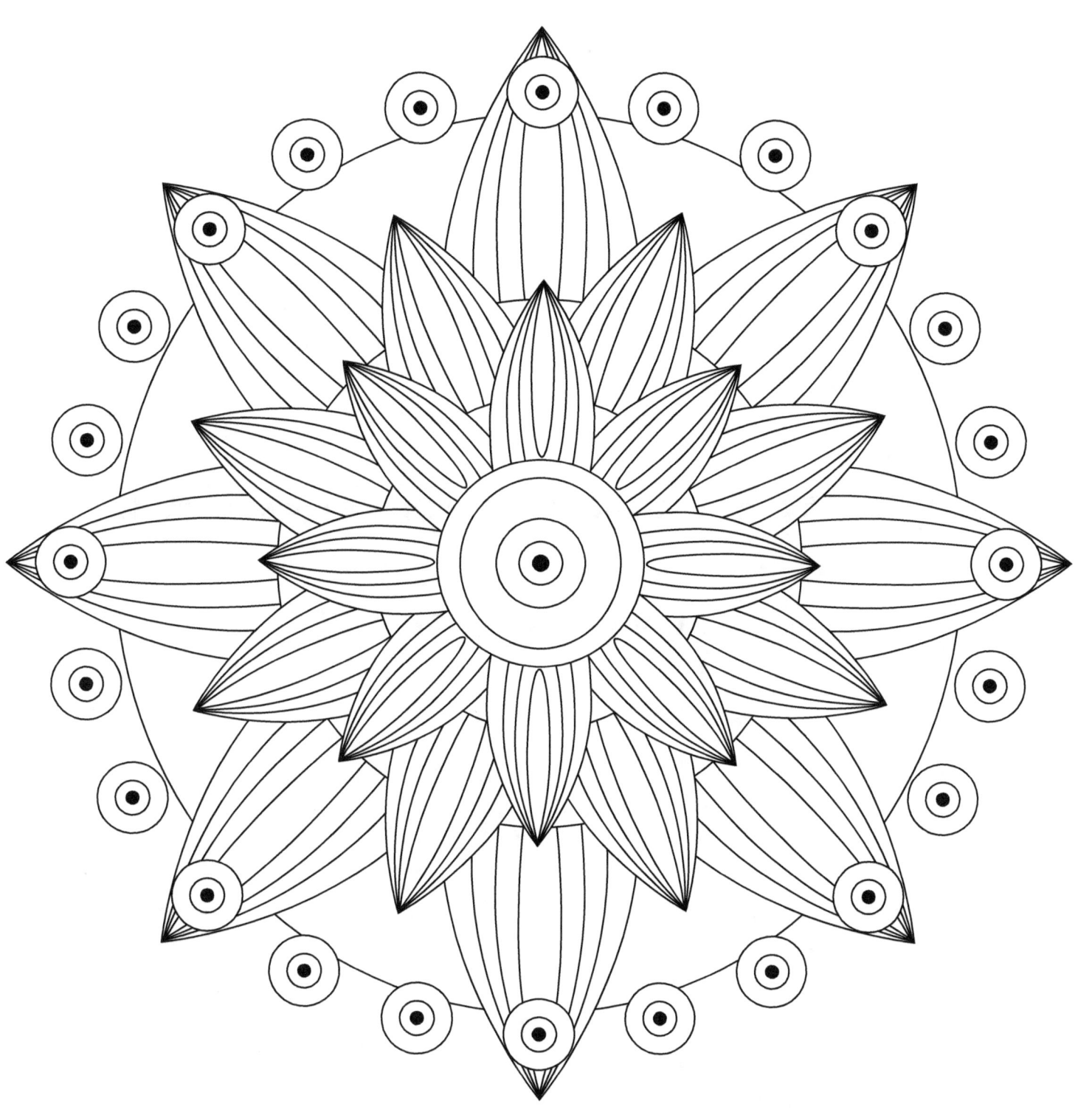

Try to be a rainbow in someone's cloud.

Maya Angelou

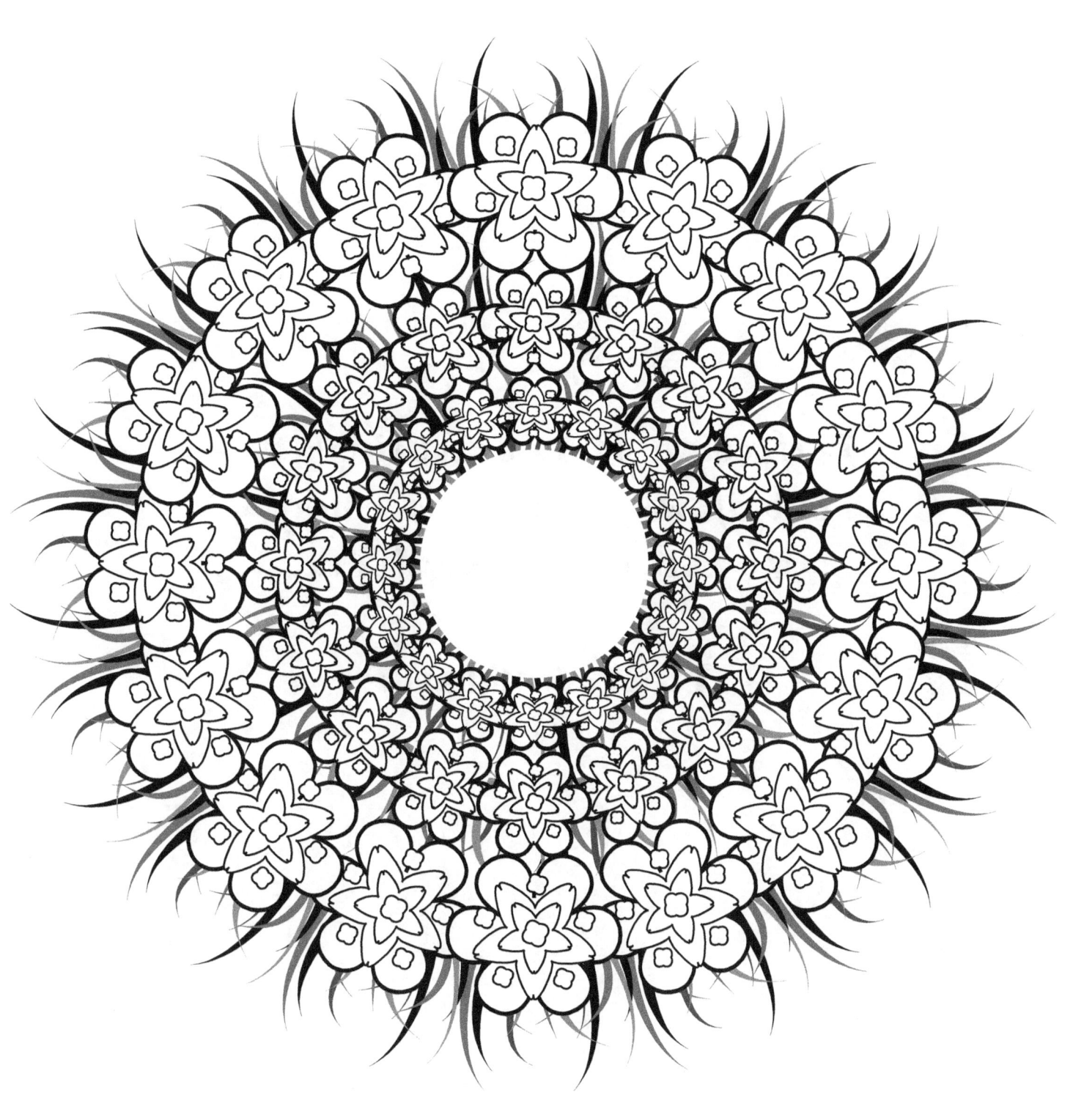

Perfection is not attainable,
but if we chase perfection
we can catch excellence.

Vince Lombardi

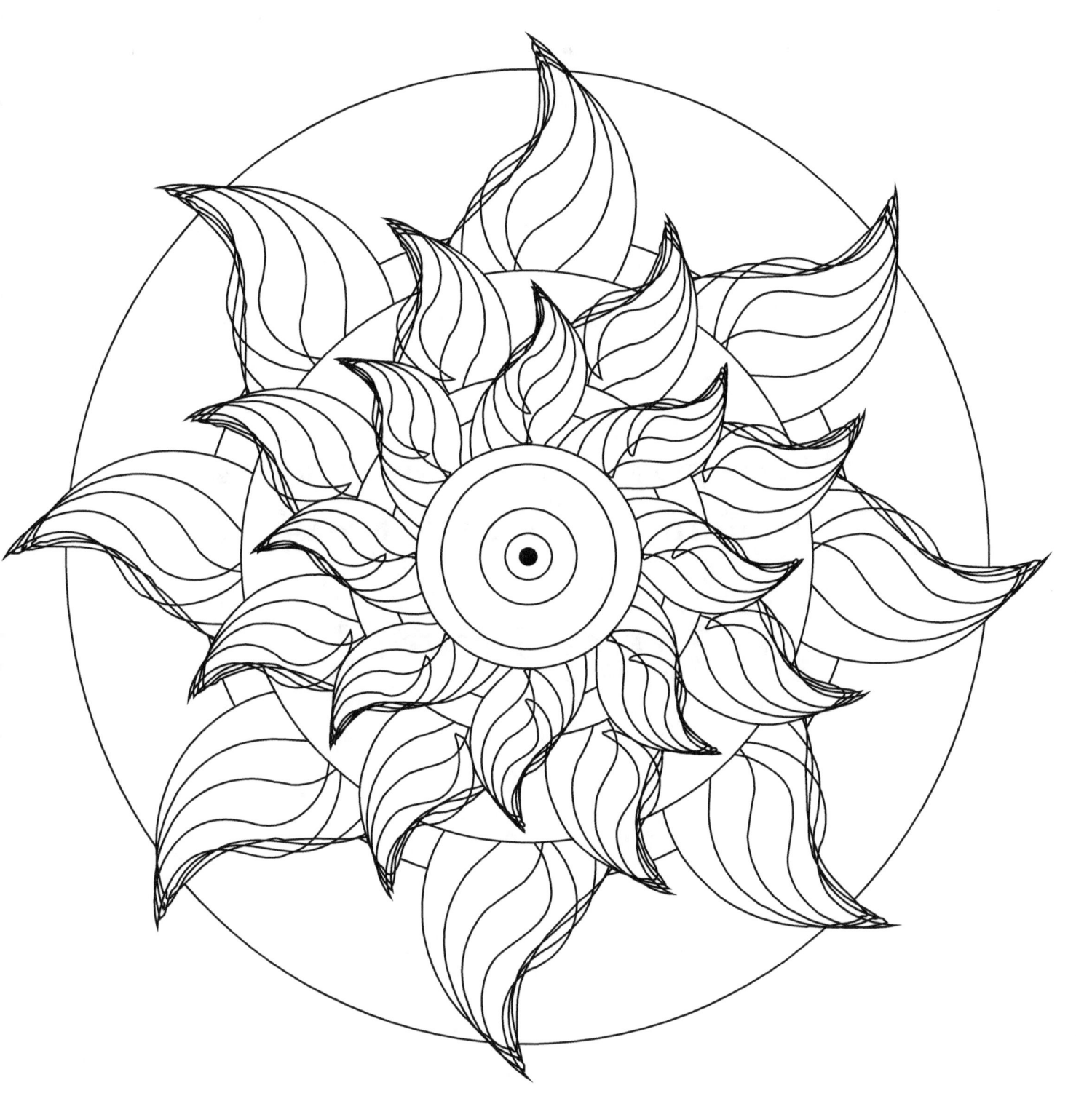

The best preparation for tomorrow
is doing your best today.

H. Jackson Brown, Jr.

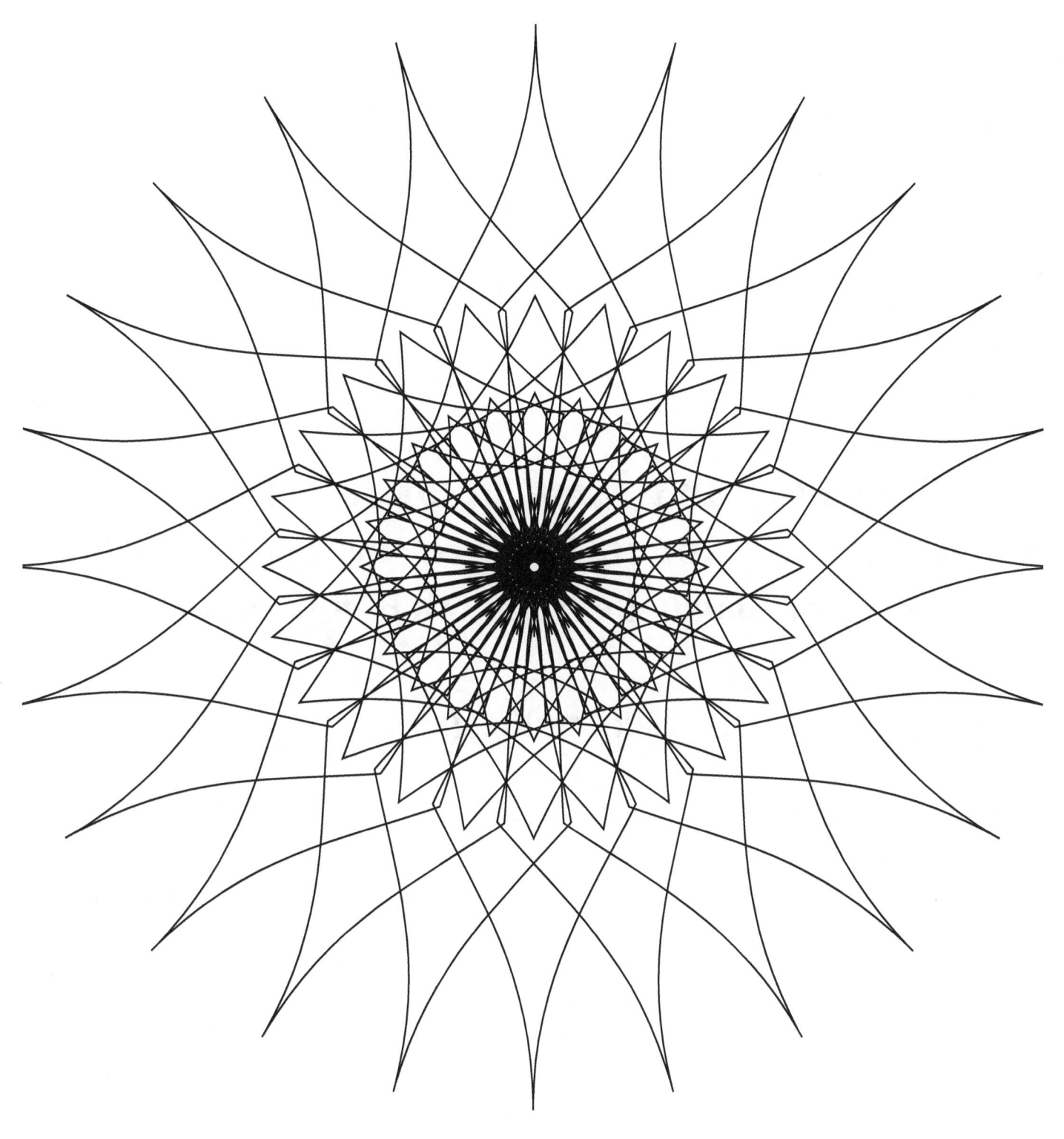

The best and most beautiful things
in the world cannot be seen or even touched
- they must be felt with the heart.

Helen Keller

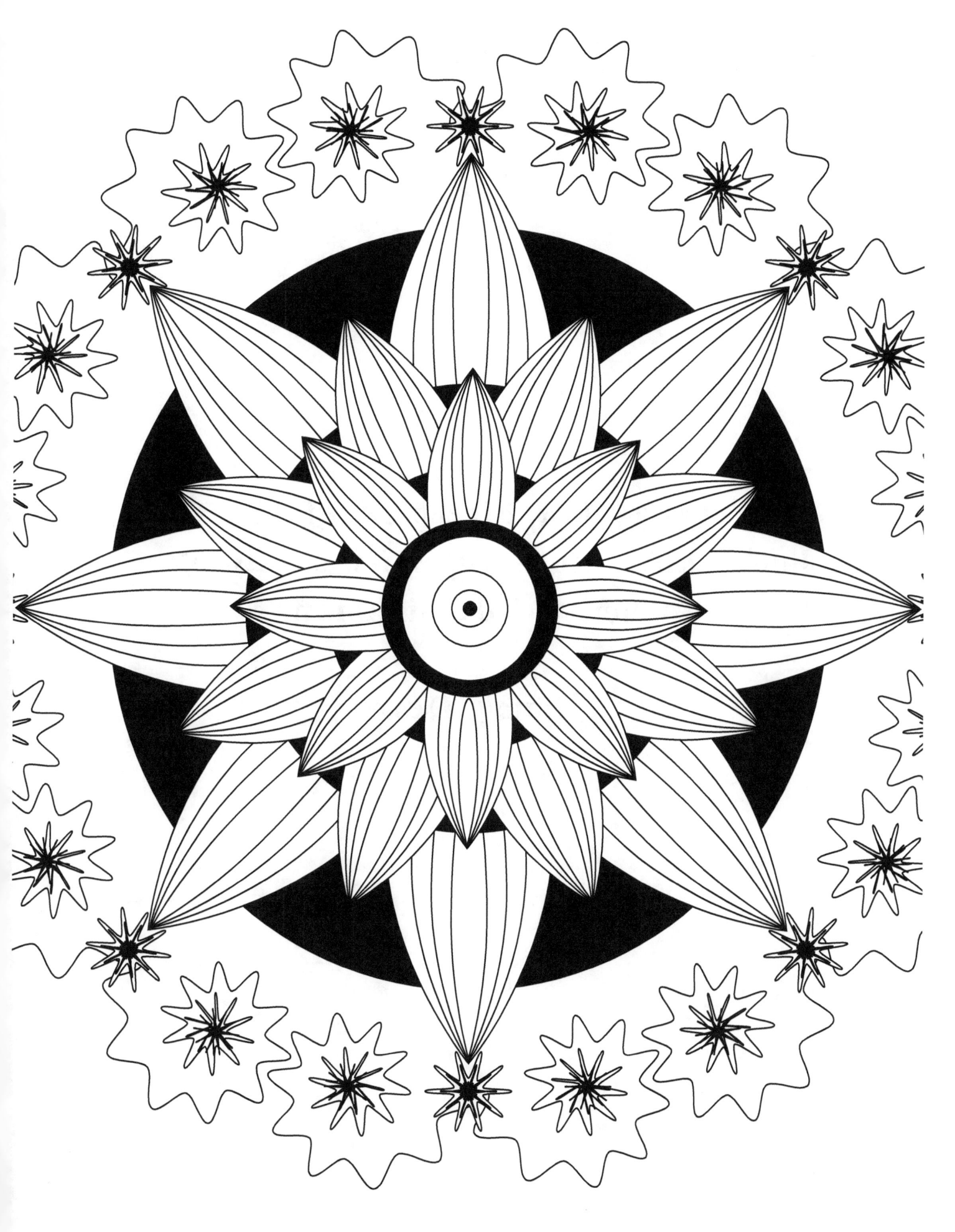

i can't change the direction of the wind,
but i can adjust my sails to always
reach my destination.

Jimmy Dean

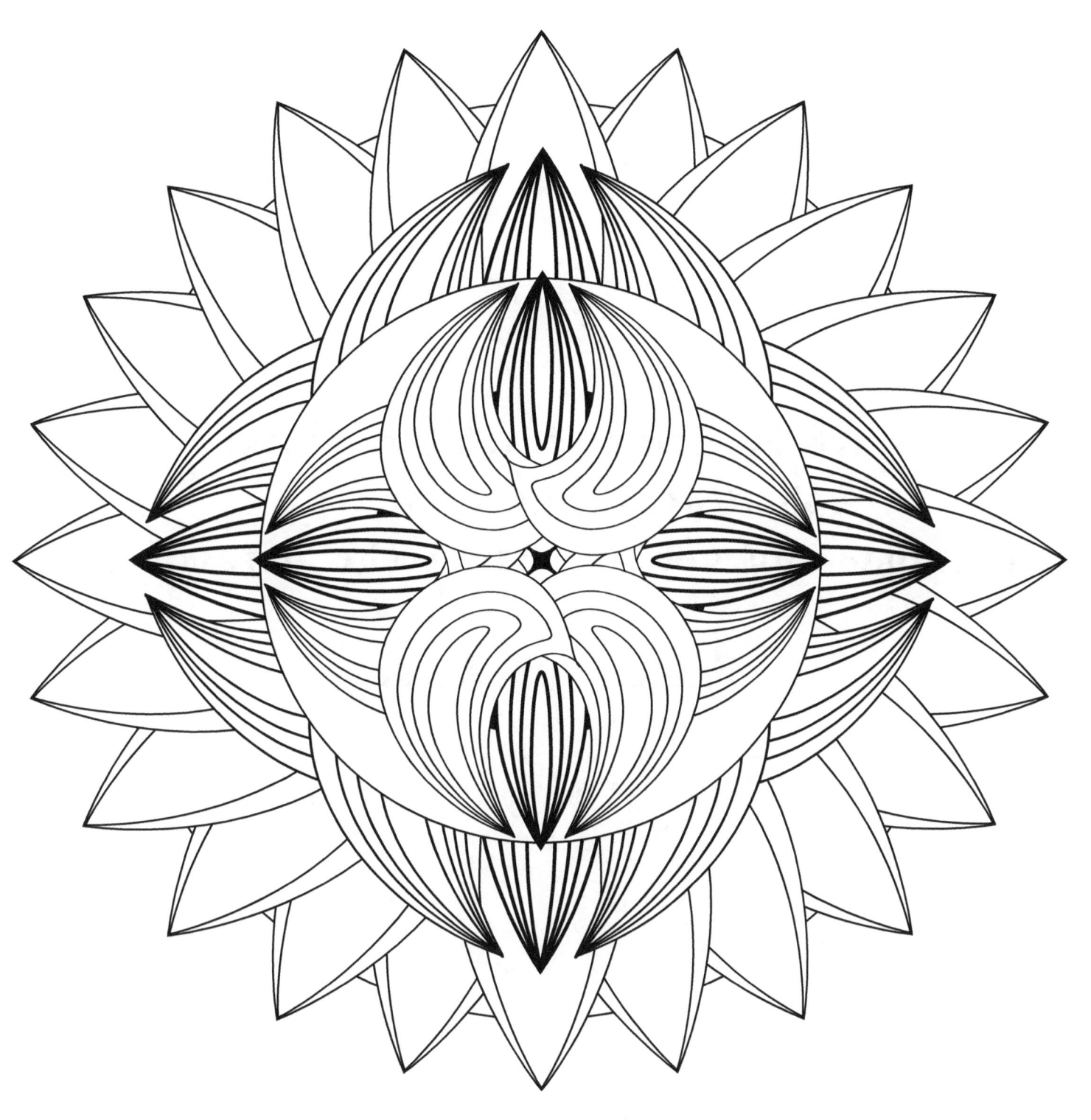

Start by doing what's necessary;
then do what's possible;
and suddenly you are doing the impossible.

Francis of Assisi

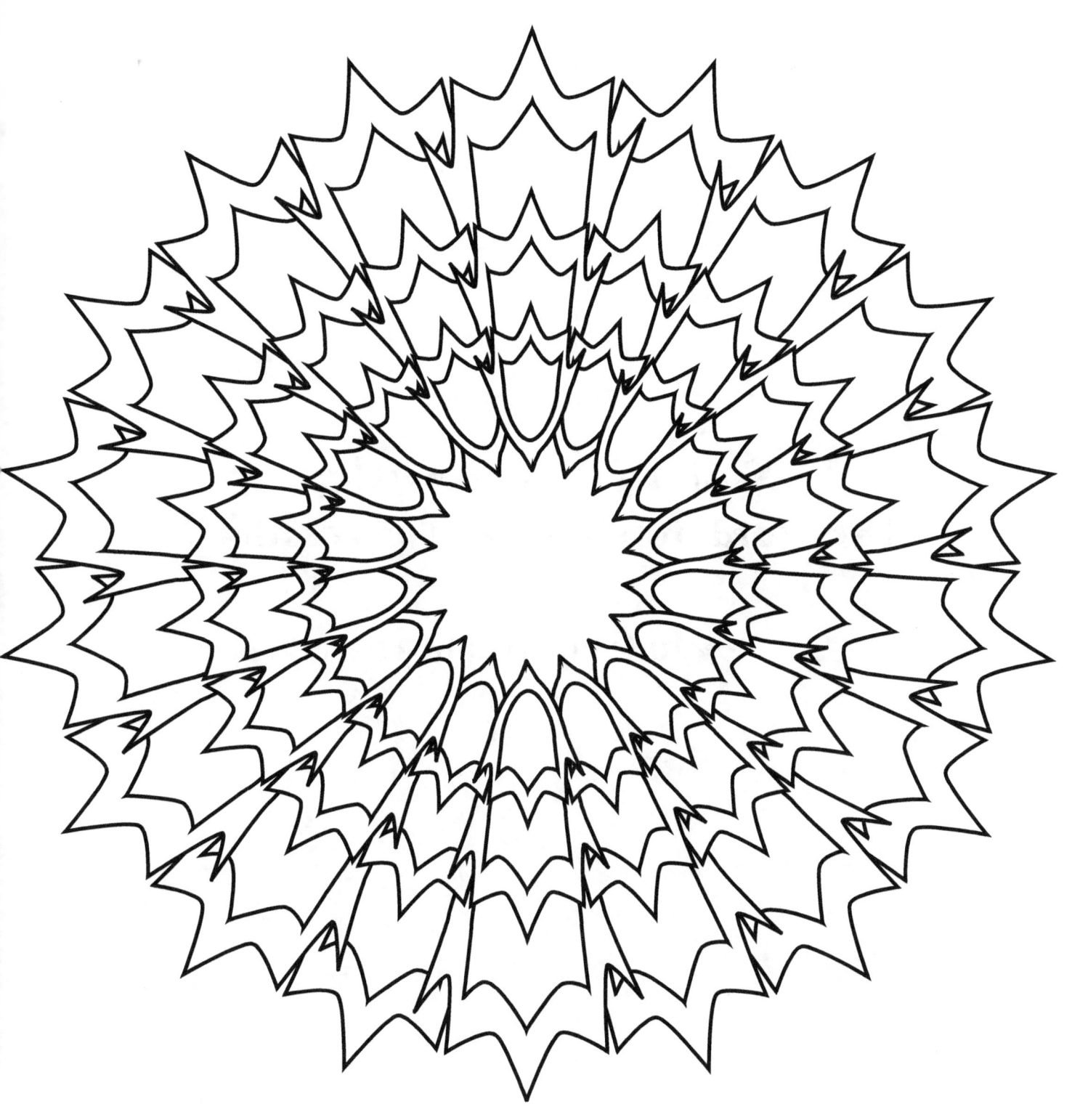

Nothing is impossible,
the word itself says "I'm possible"!

Audrey Hepburn

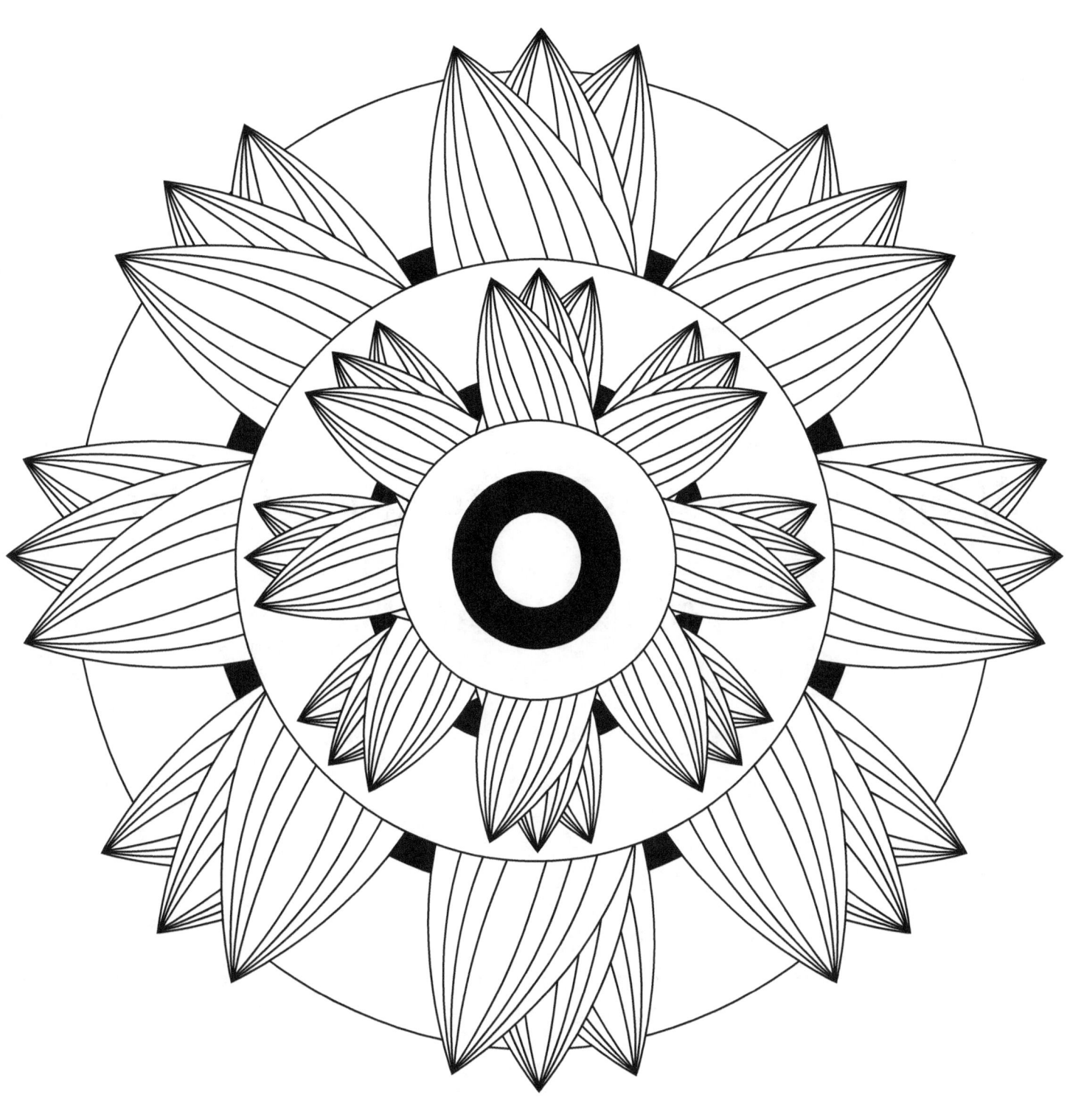

If opportunity doesn't knock, build a door.

Milton Berle

_____

_____

_____

_____

_____

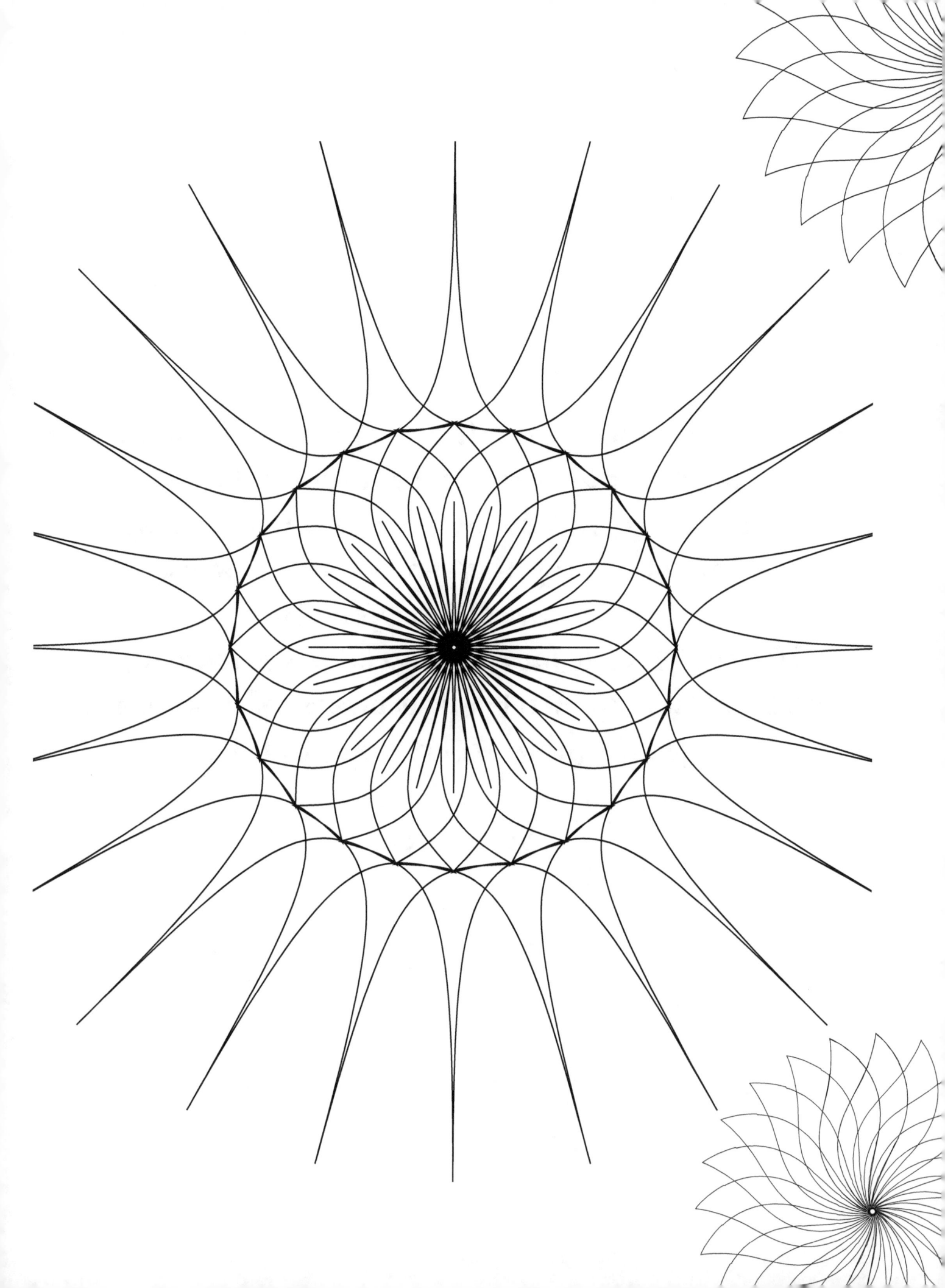

Your work is going to fill a large part of your life,
and the only way to be truly satisfied
is to do what you believe is great work.
And the only way to do great work
is to love what you do.
If you haven't found it yet, keep looking.
Don't settle. As with all matters of the heart,
you'll know when you find it.

Steve Jobs

_____

_____

_____

_____

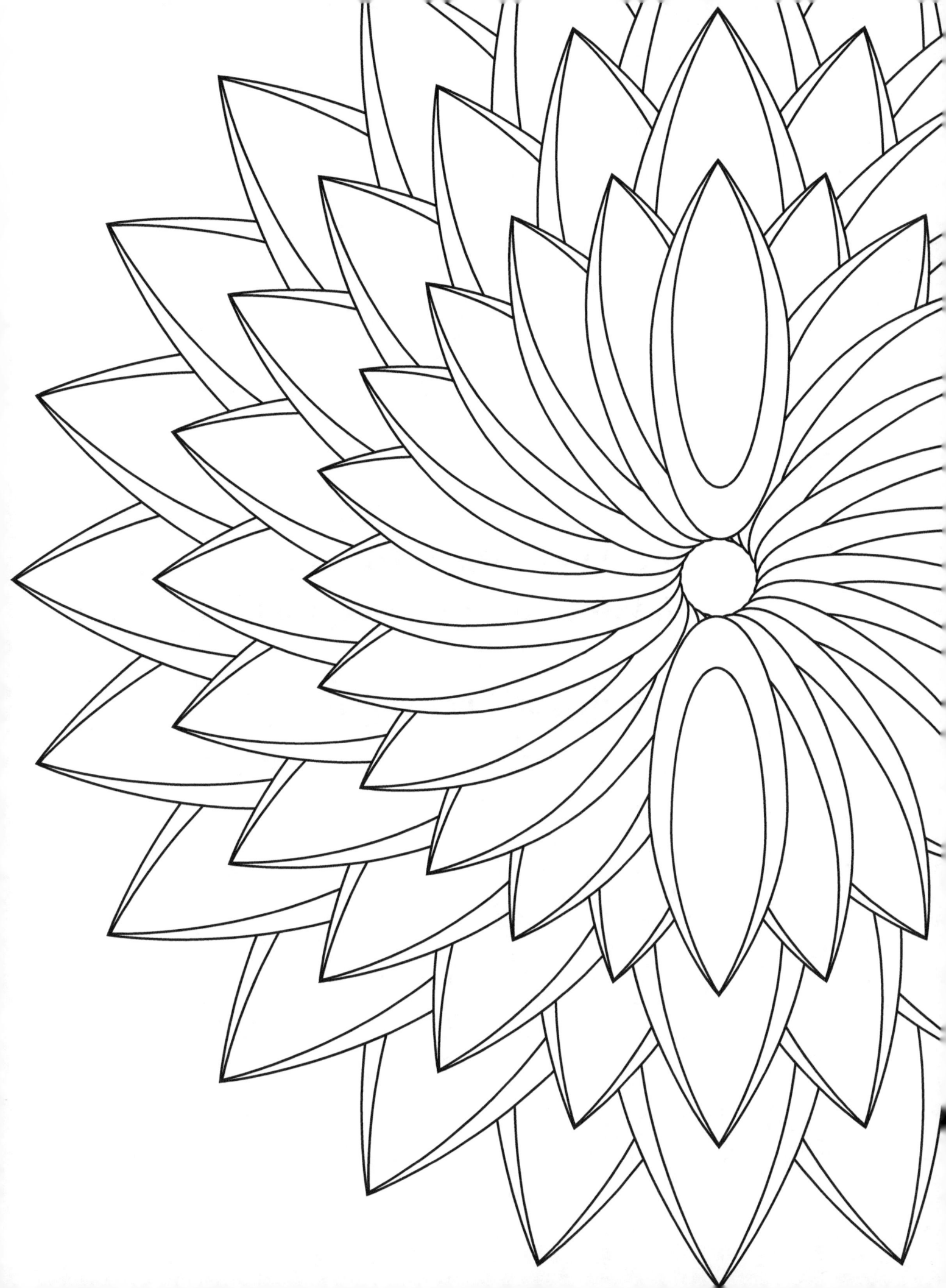

We know what we are,
but know not what we may be.

William Shakespeare

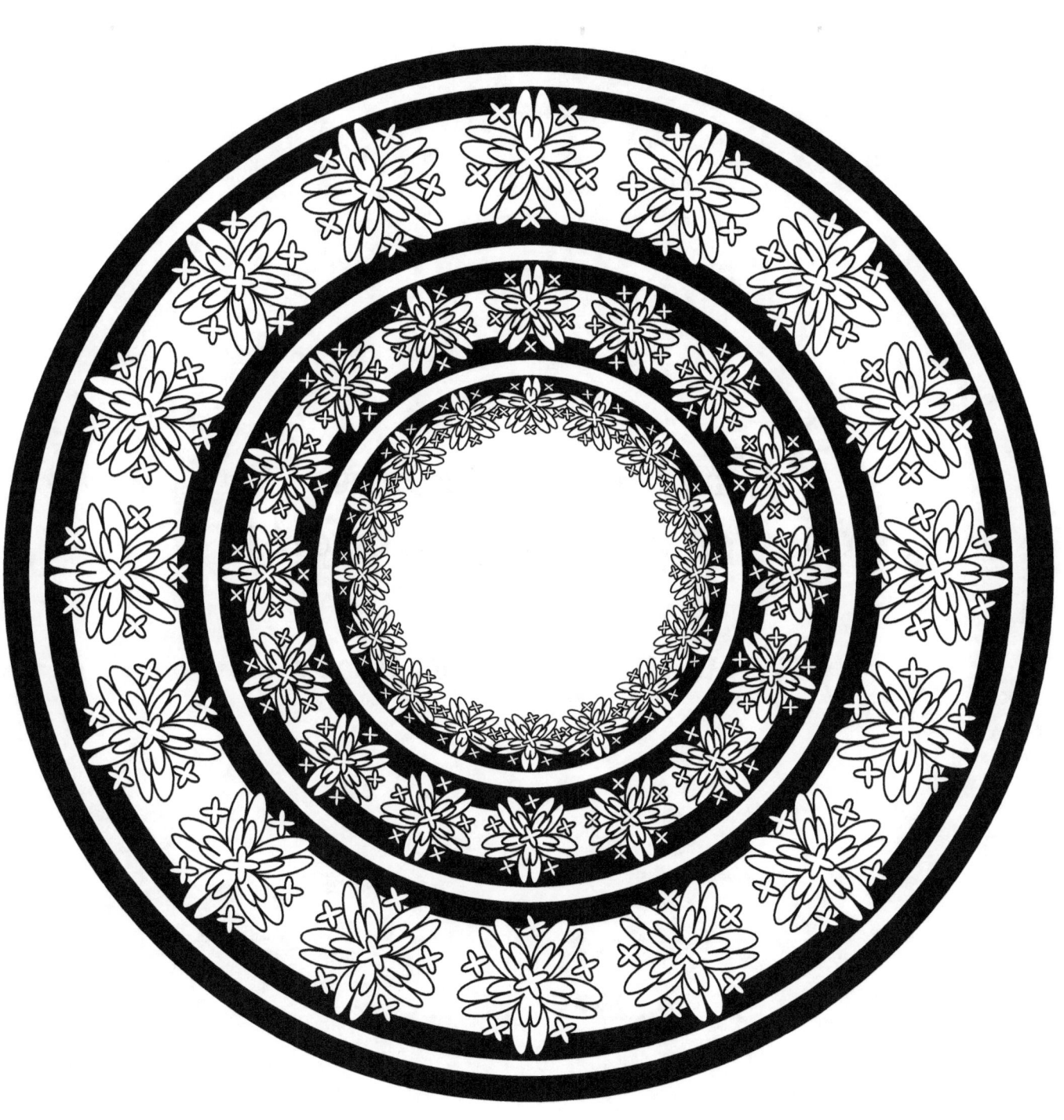

Change your thoughts
and you change your world.

Norman Vincent Peale

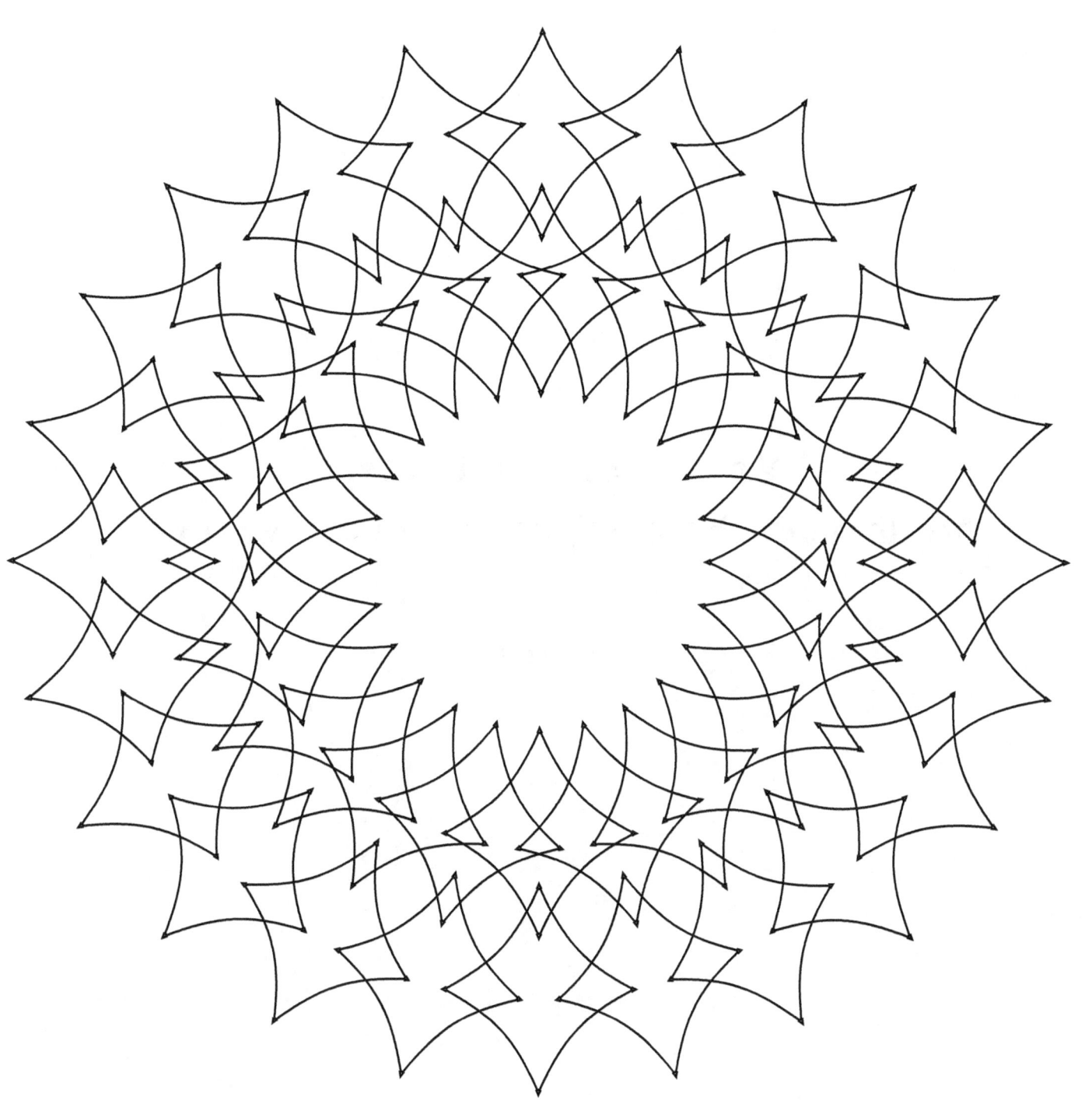

No act of kindness,
no matter how small, is ever wasted.

Aesop

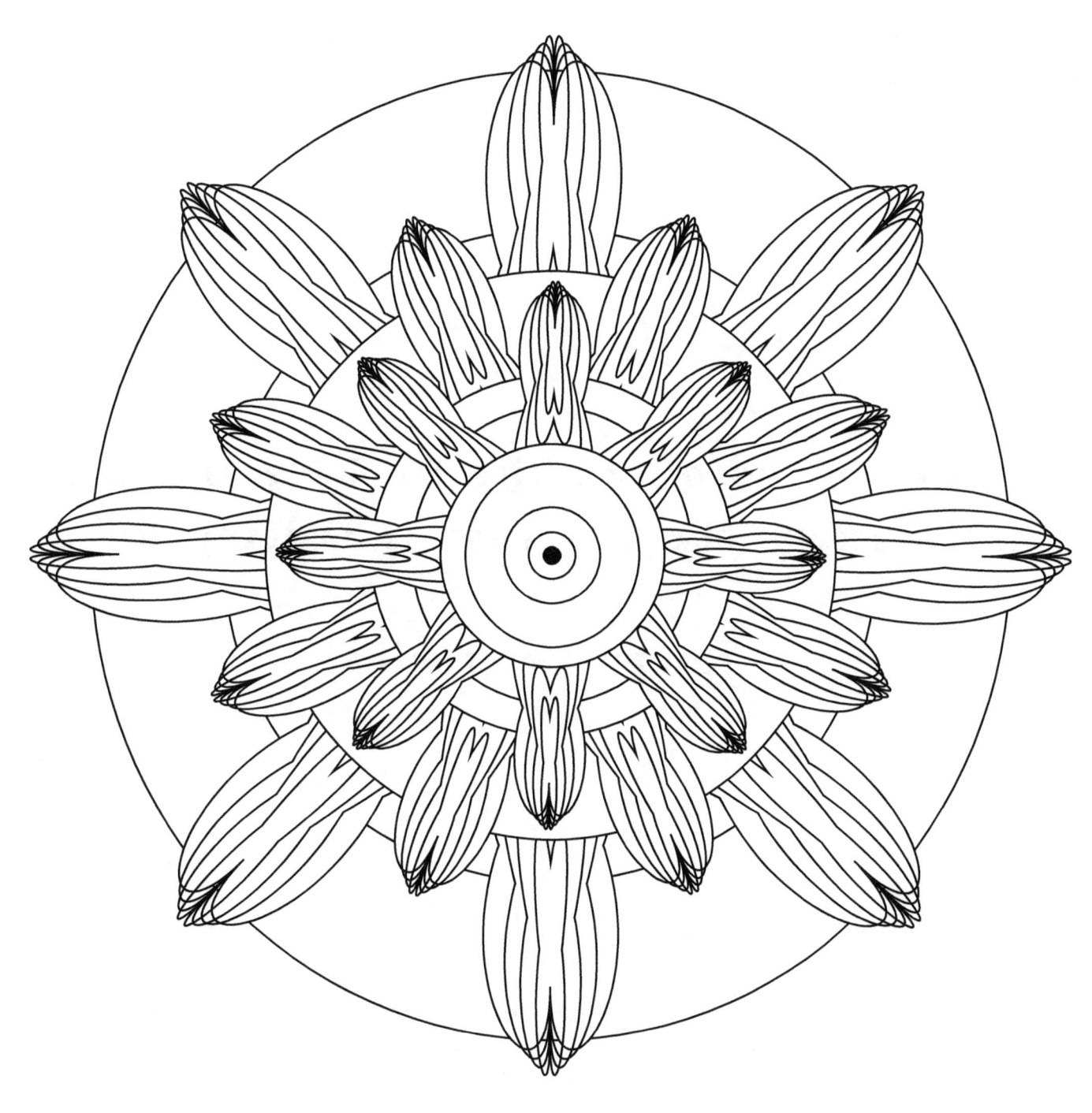

We must let go of the life we have planned,
so as to accept the one that is waiting for us.

Joseph Campbell

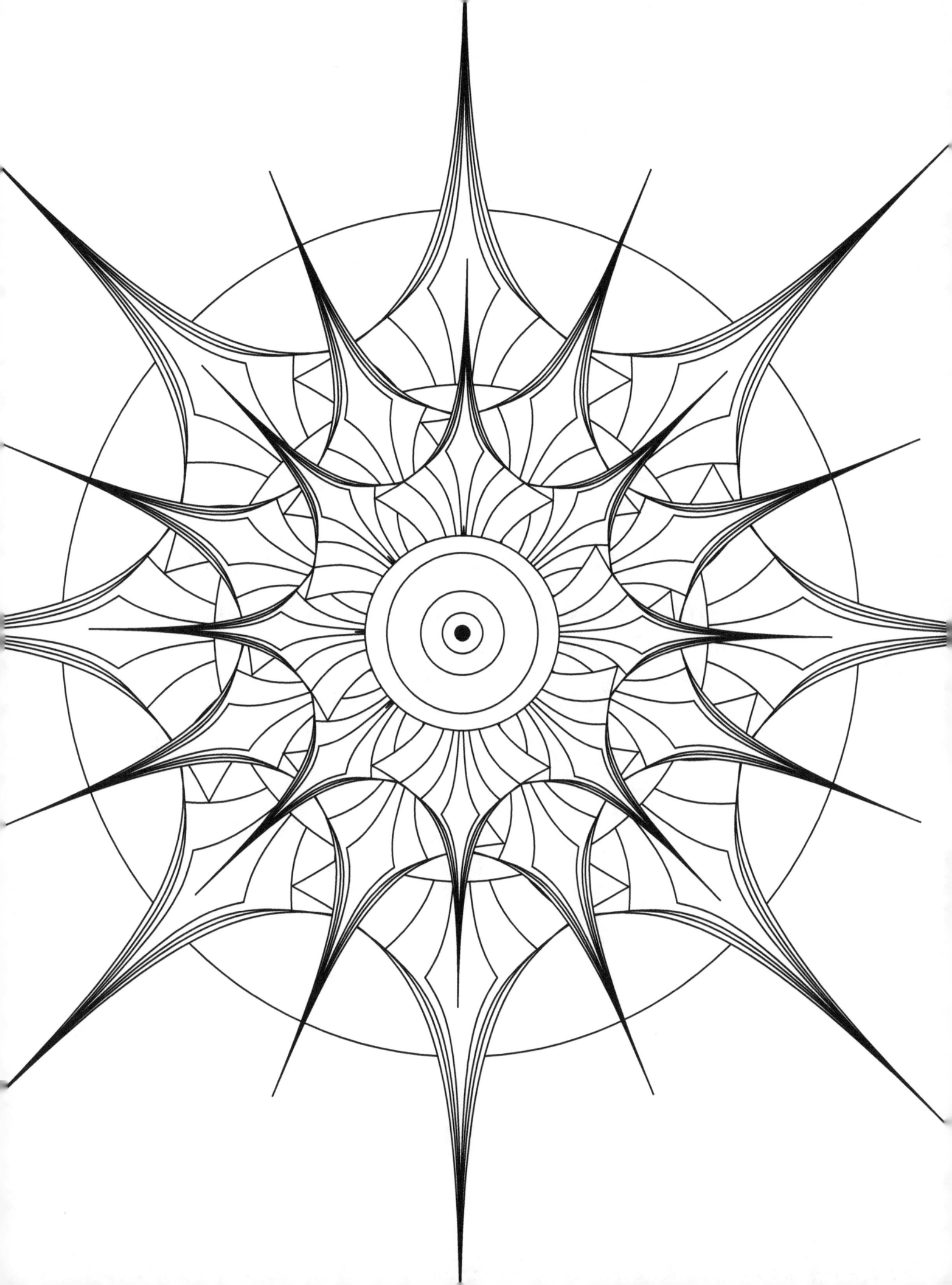

It is during our darkest moments
that we must focus to see the light.

Aristotle Onassis

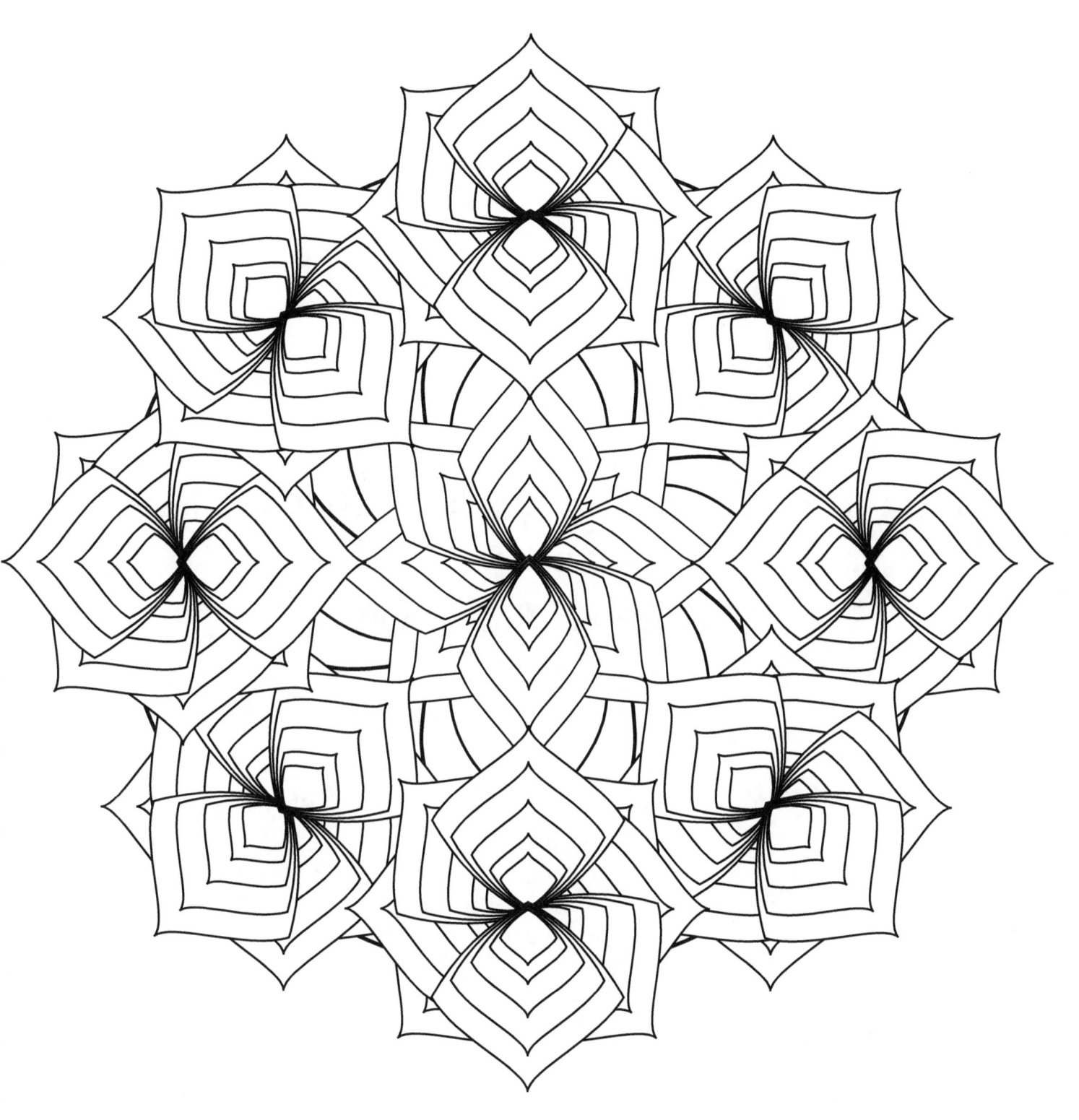

Believe you can and you're halfway there.

Theodore Roosevelt

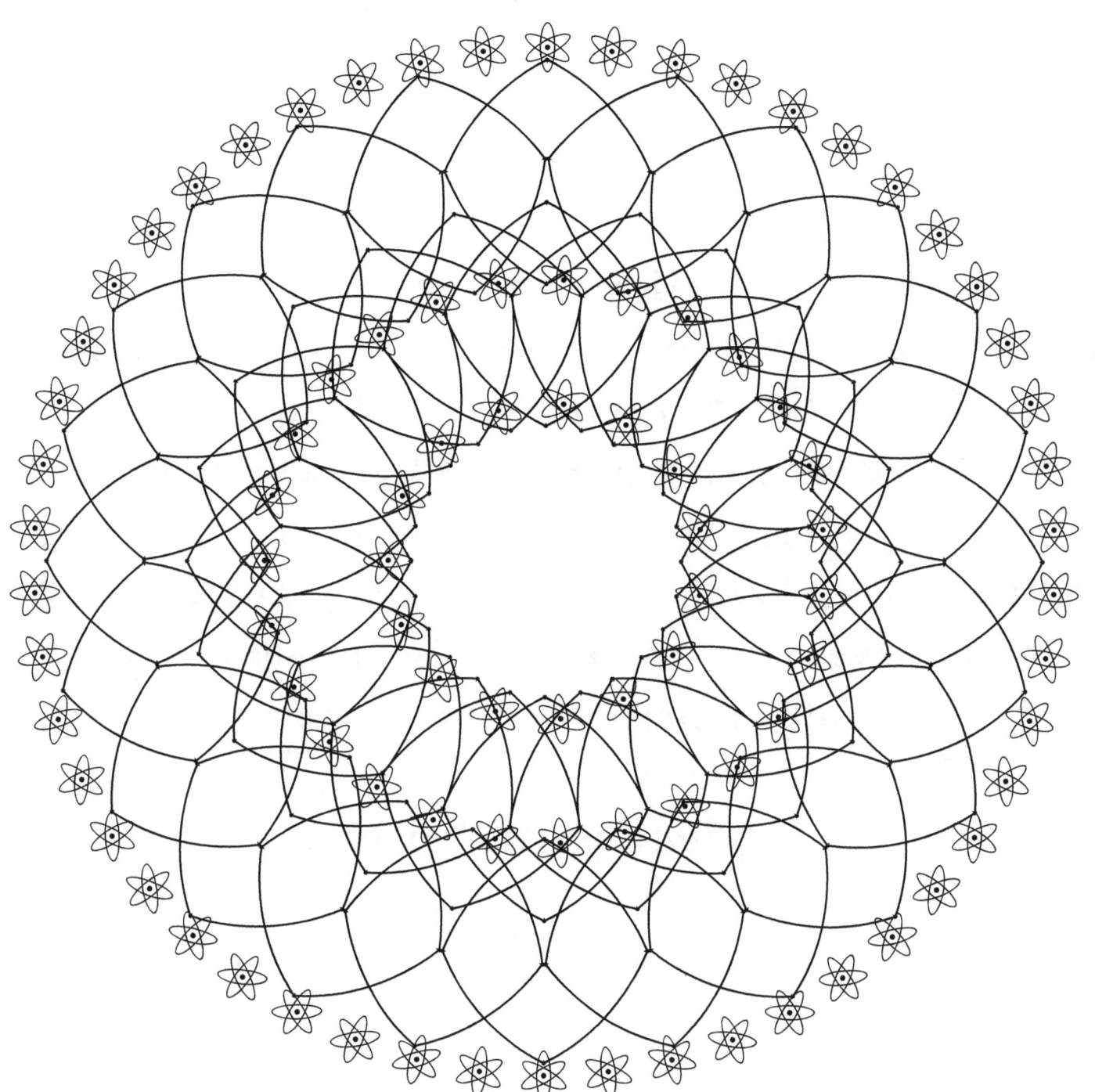

i believe in pink.
i believe that laughing is the best calorie burner.
i believe in kissing, kissing a lot.
i believe in being strong when everything
seems to be going wrong.
i believe that happy girls are the prettiest girls.
i believe that tomorrow is another day
and i believe in miracles.

Audrey Hepburn

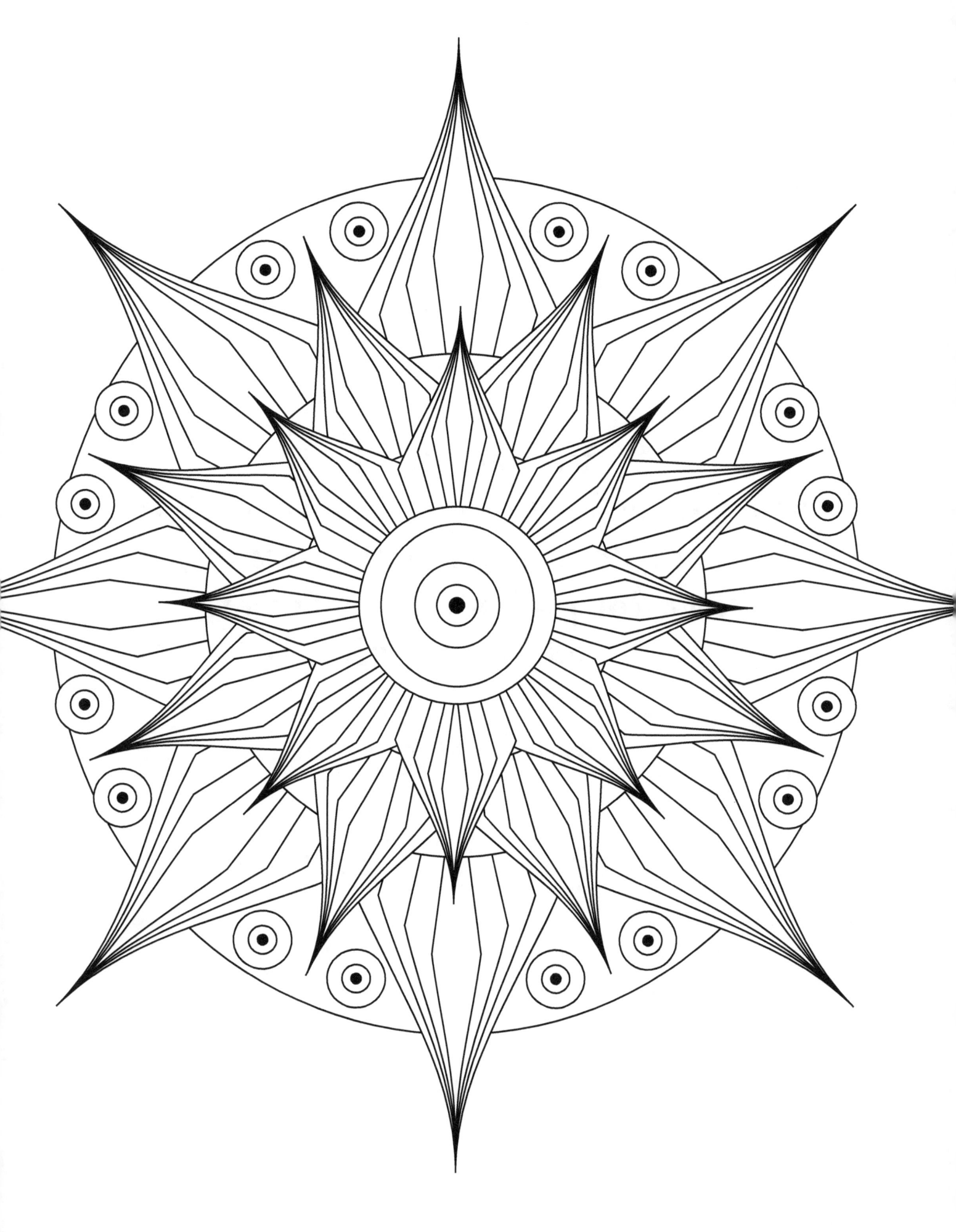

My mission in life is
not merely to survive, but to thrive;
and to do so with some passion,
some compassion, some humor,
and some style.

Maya Angelou

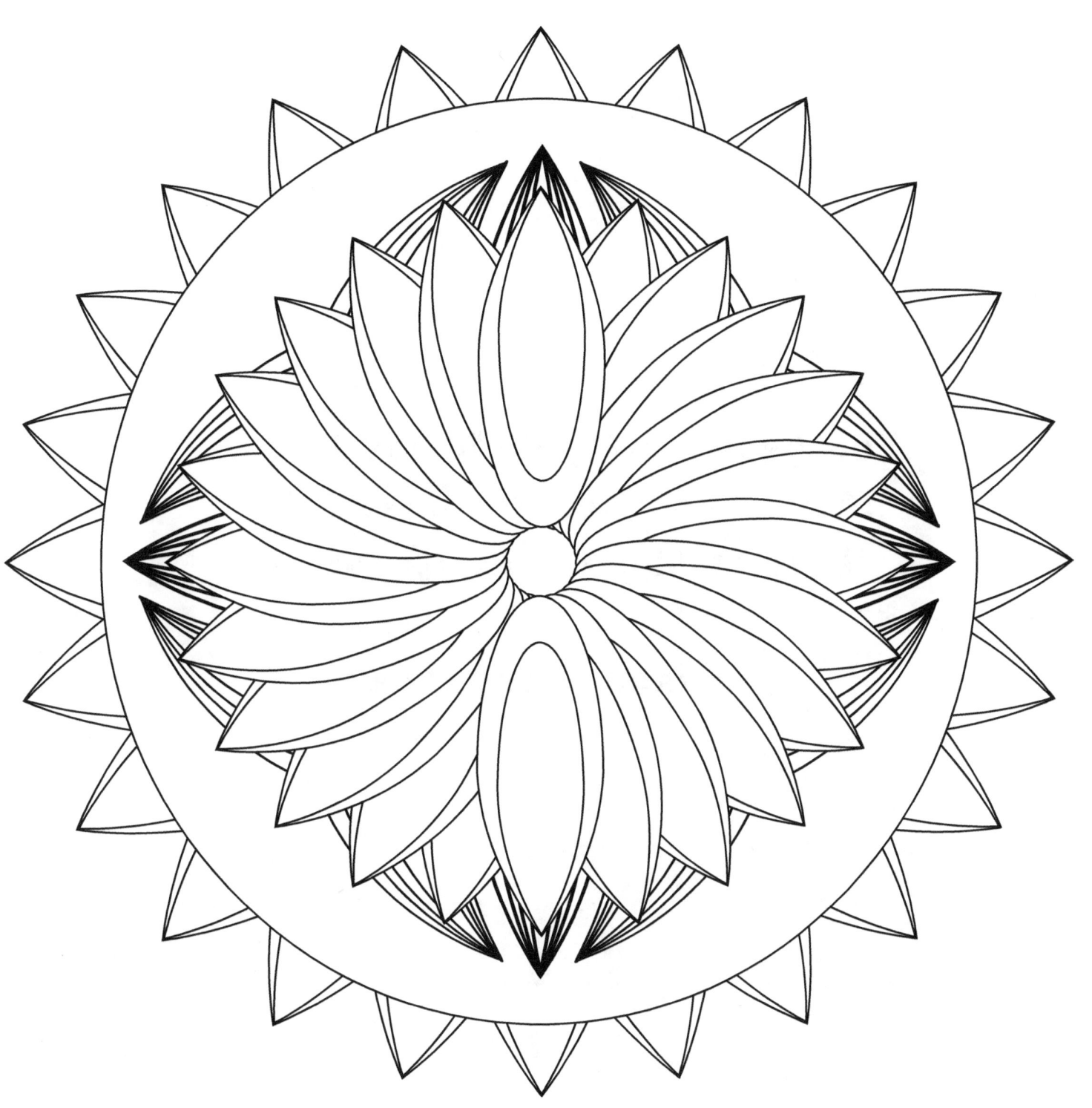

Put your heart, mind, and soul
into even your smallest acts.
This is the secret of success.

Swami Sivananda

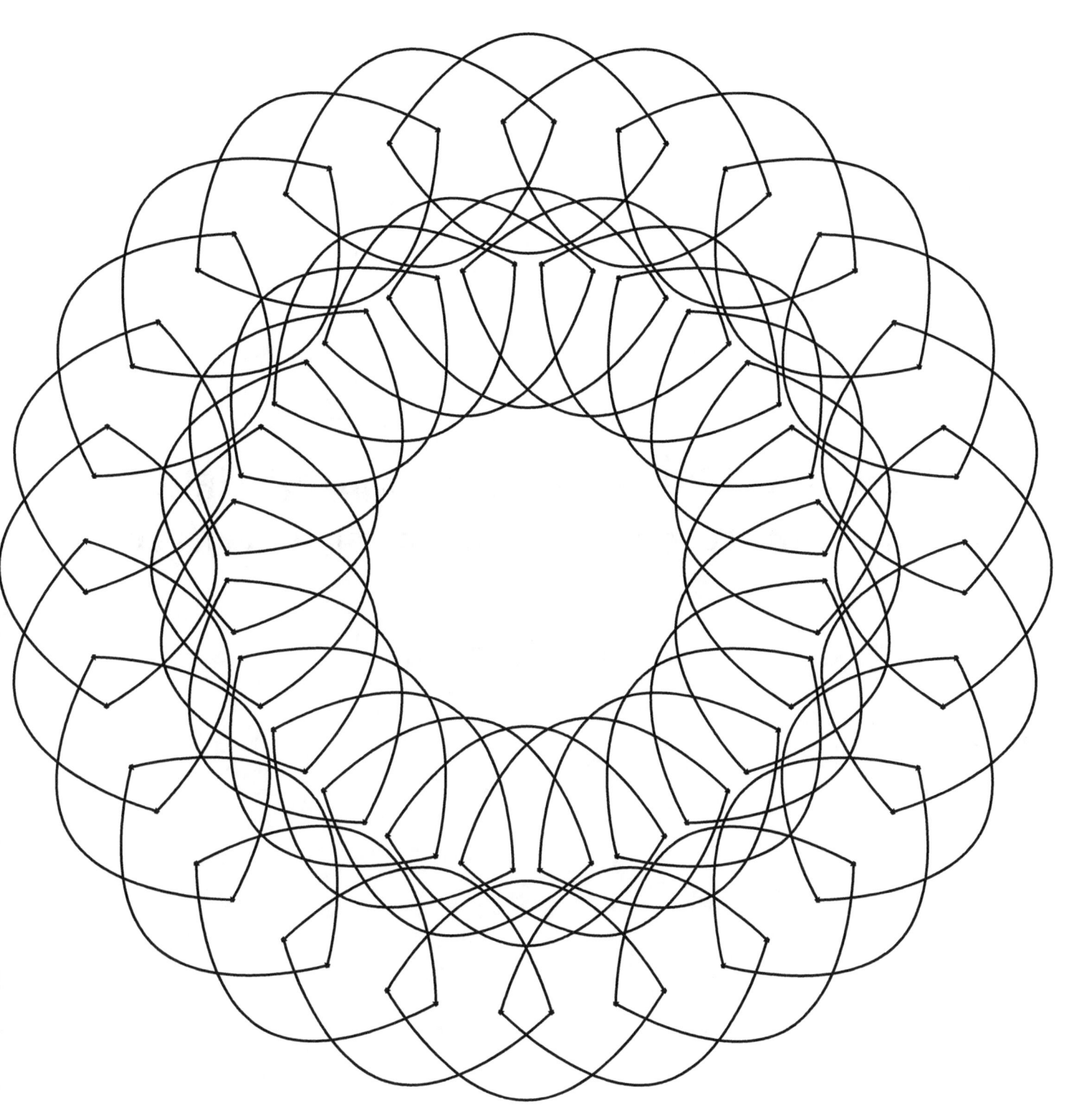

There are two ways of spreading light:
to be the candle or the mirror that reflects it.

Edith Wharton

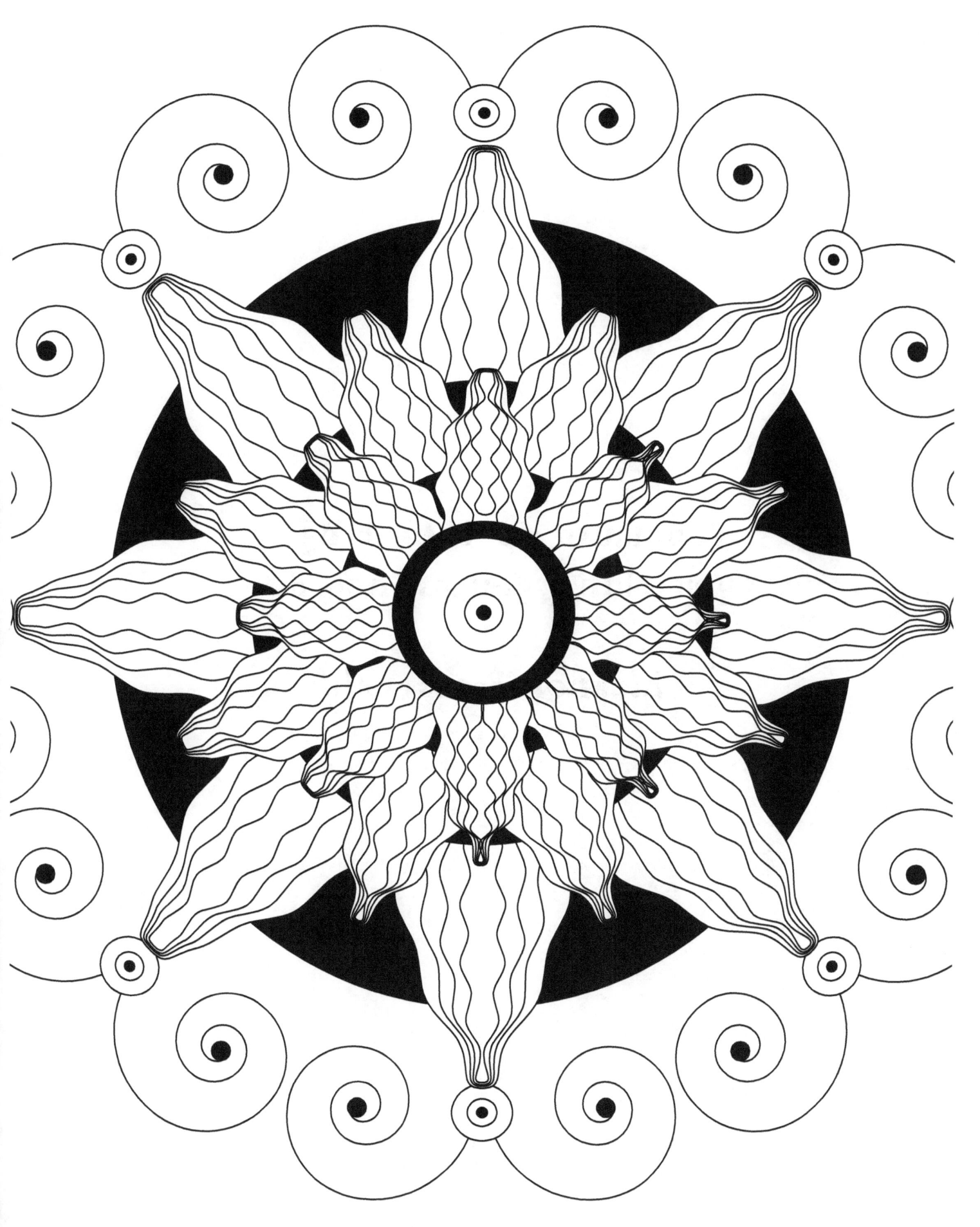

You must do the things
you think you cannot do.

Eleanor Roosevelt

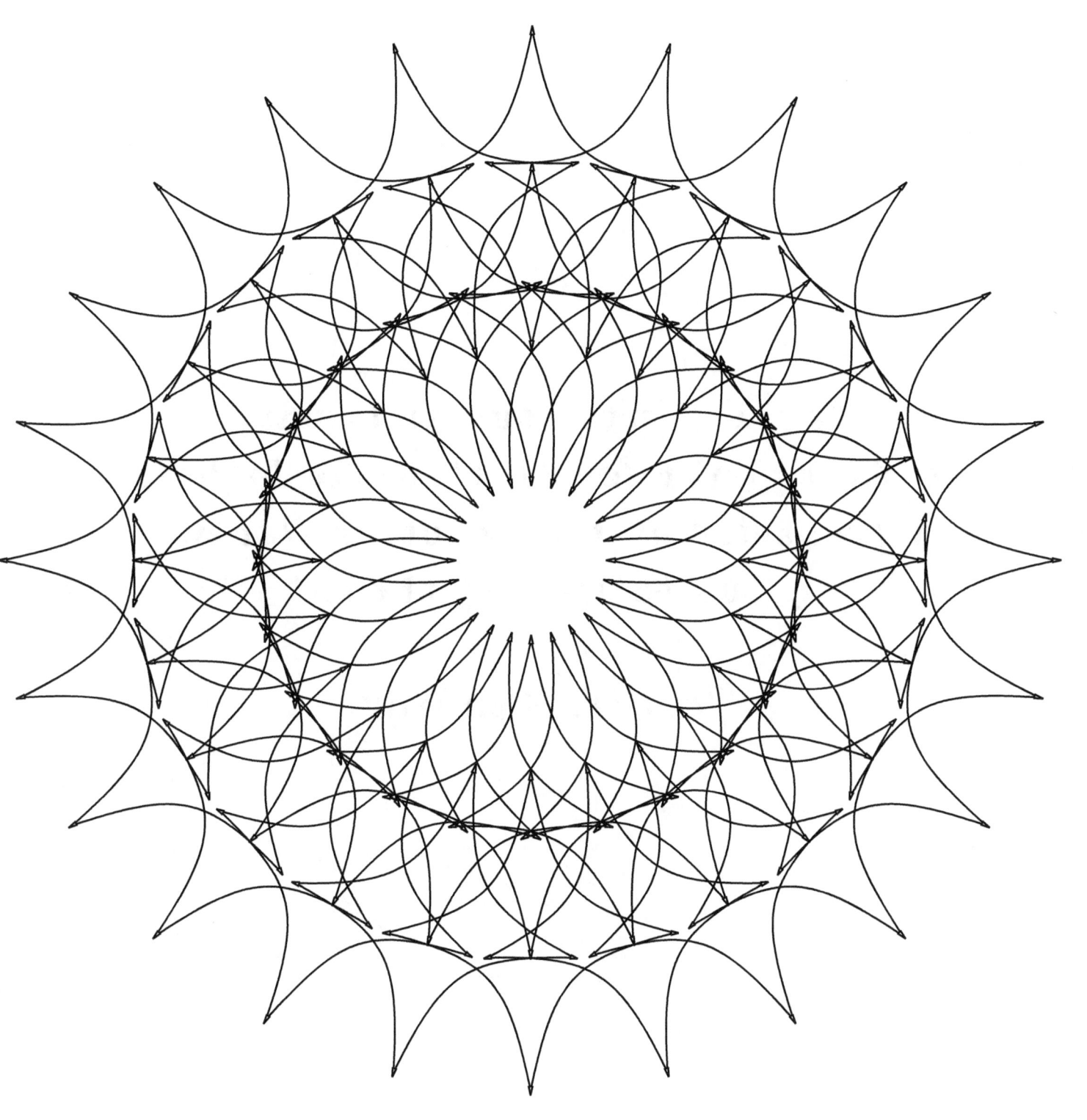

As we express our gratitude,
we must never forget that the highest
appreciation is not to utter words,
but to live by them.

John F. Kennedy

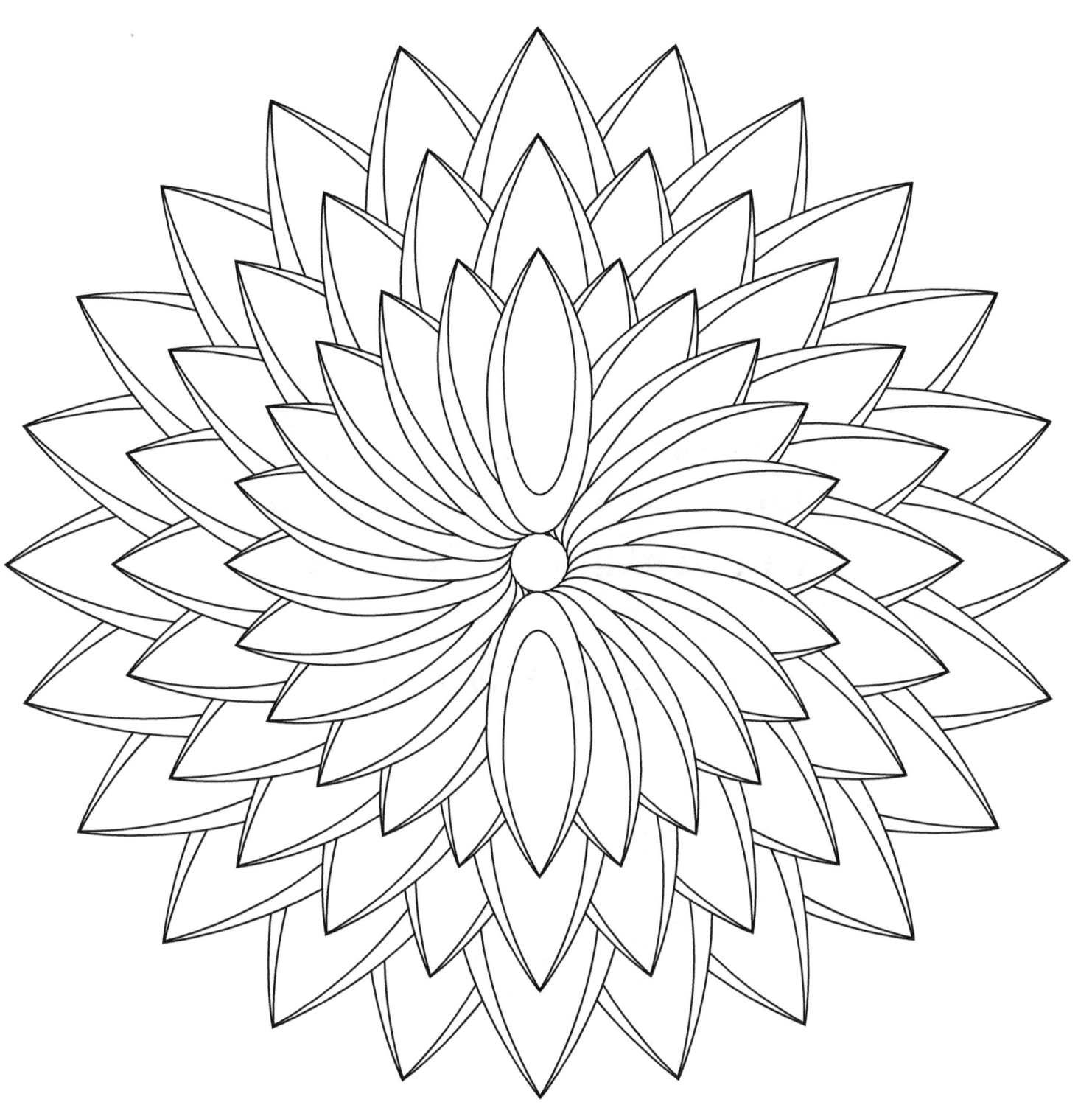

Memories of our lives,
of our works and our deeds
will continue in others.

Rosa Parks

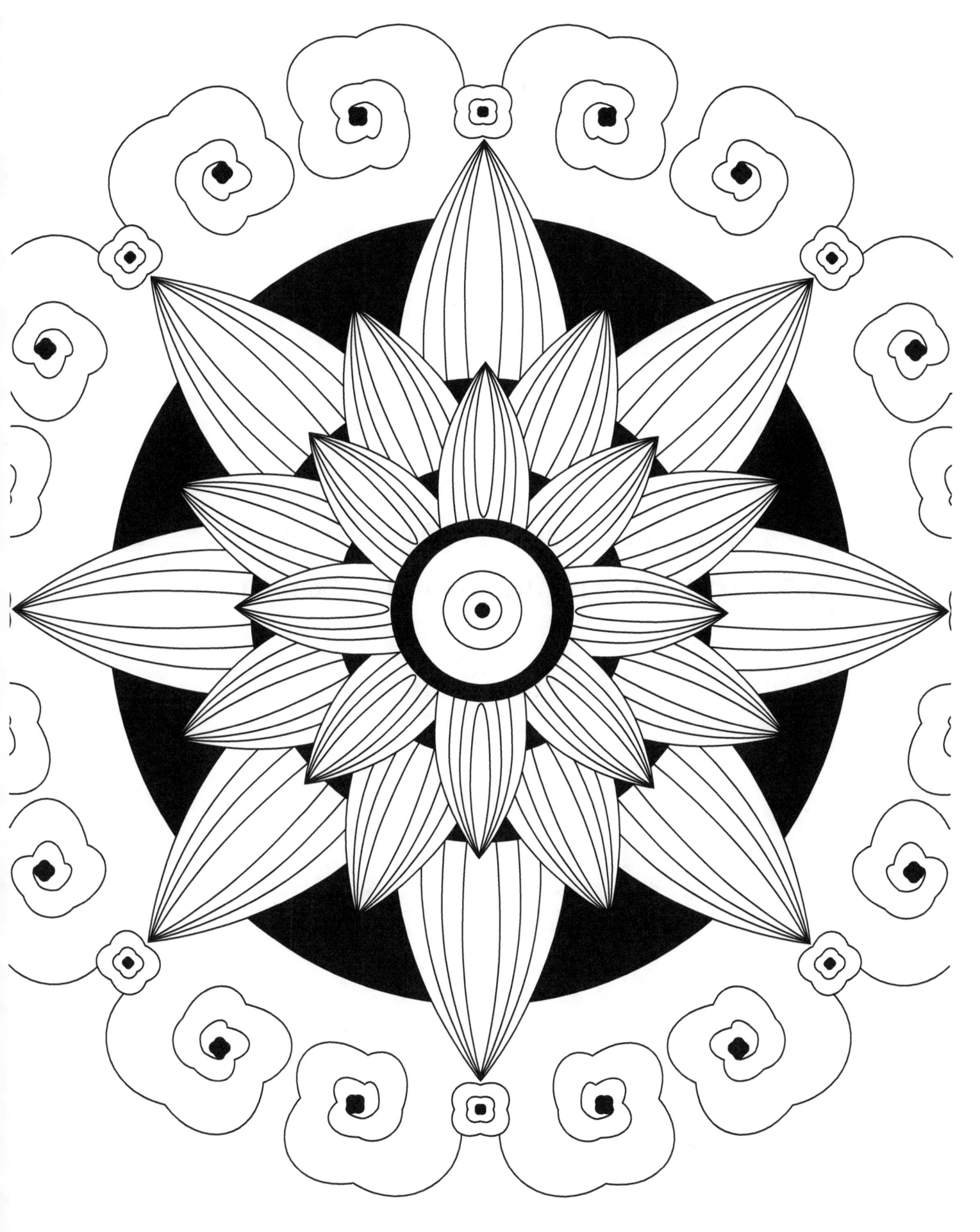

I believe in living today.
Not in yesterday, nor in tomorrow.

Loretta Young

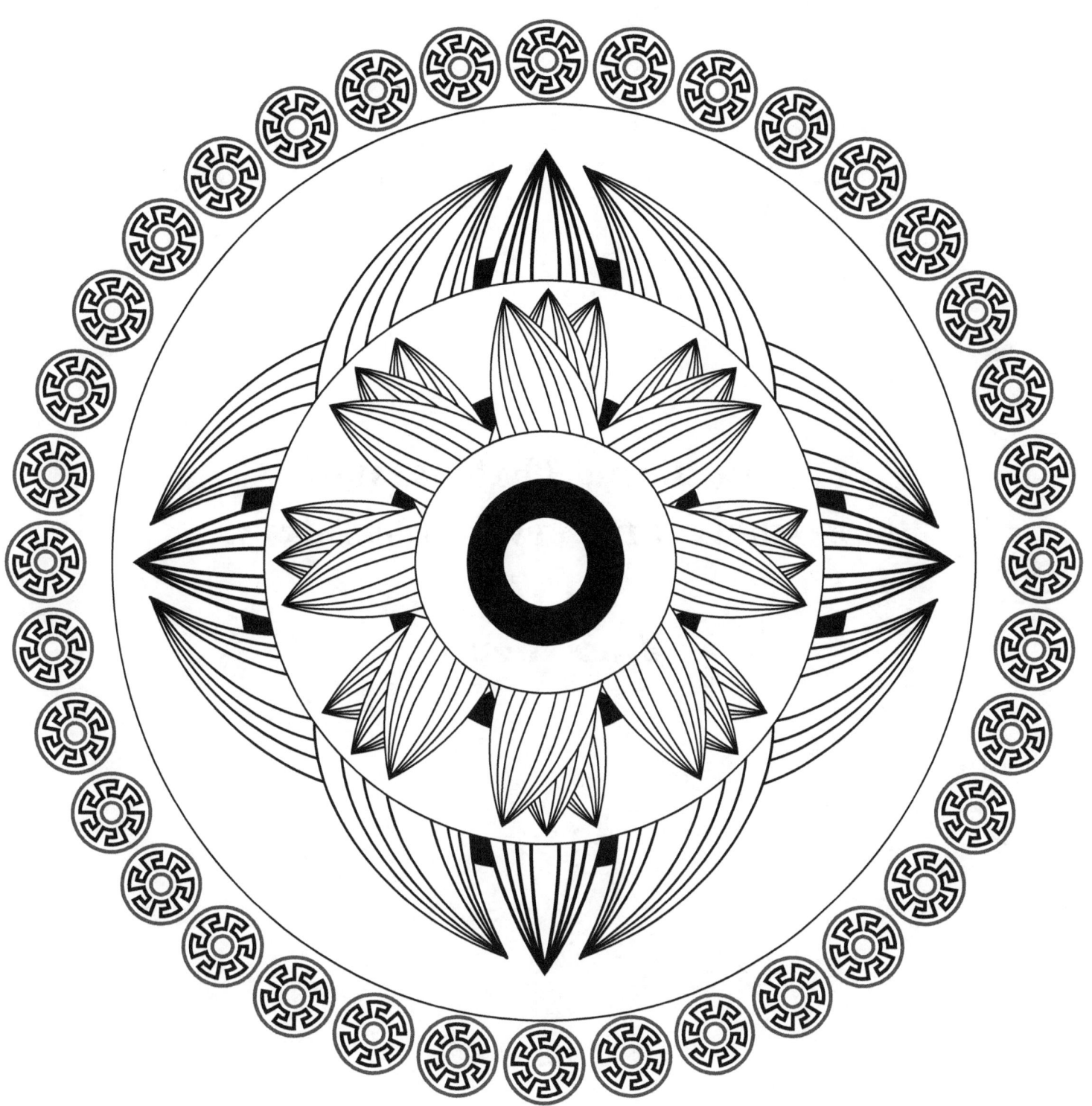

To the mind that is still,
the whole universe surrenders.

Lao Tzu

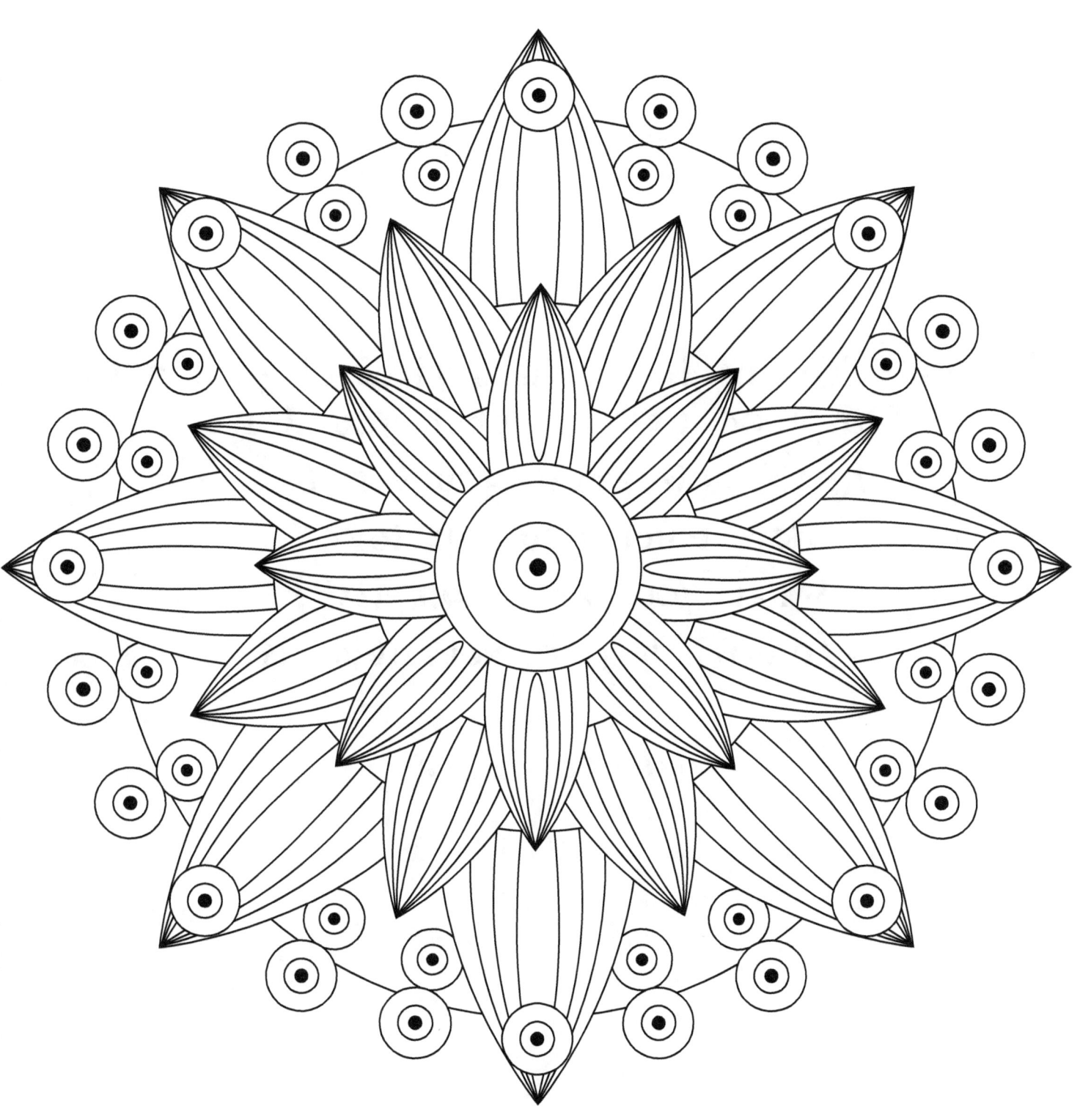

Everyone has inside of him a piece of good news.
The good news is that you don't
know how great you can be!
How much you can love!
What you can accomplish!
And what your potential is!

Anne Frank

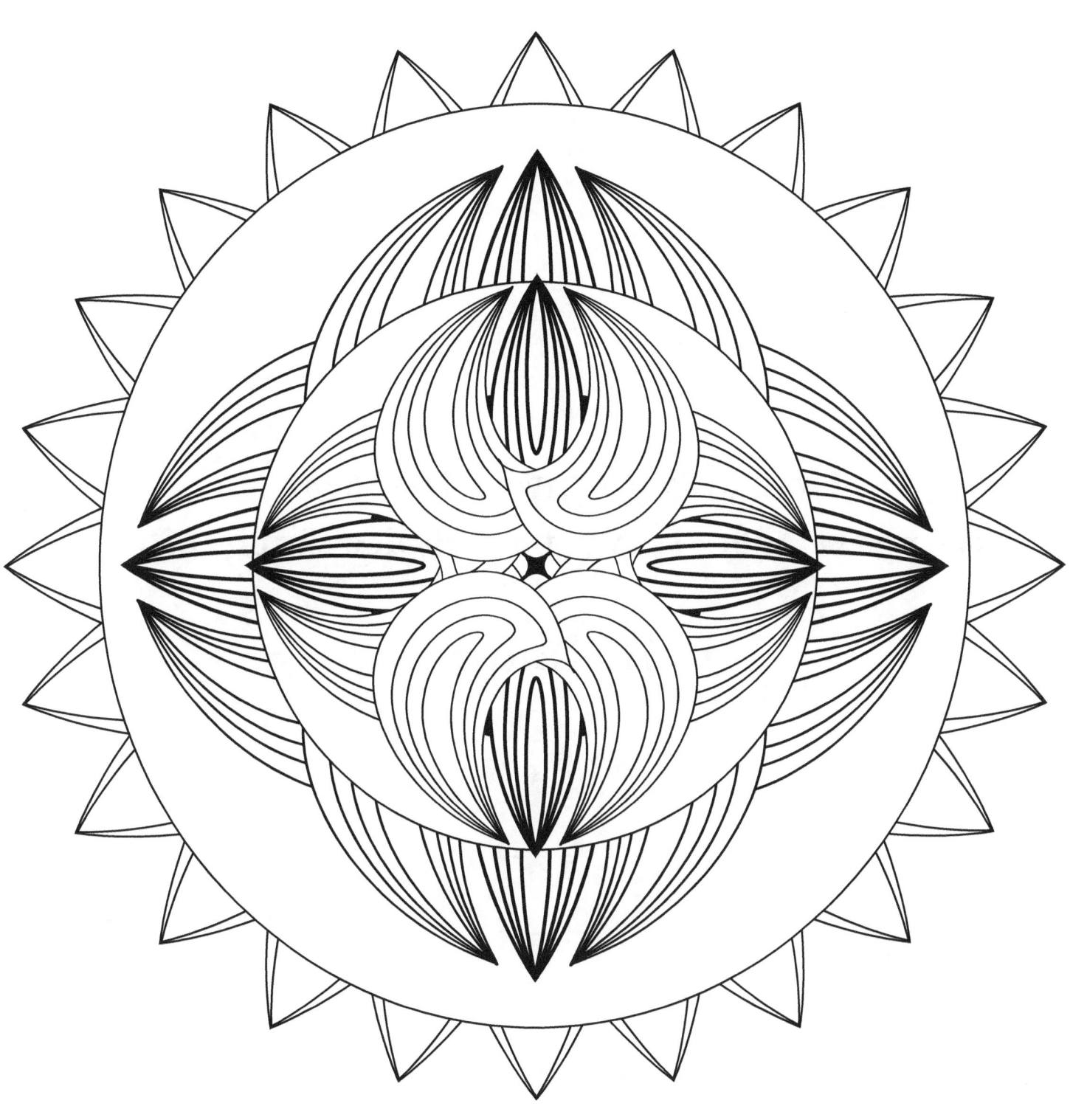

God always gives His best
to those who leave the choice with him.

Jim Elliot

_____

_____

_____

_____

_____

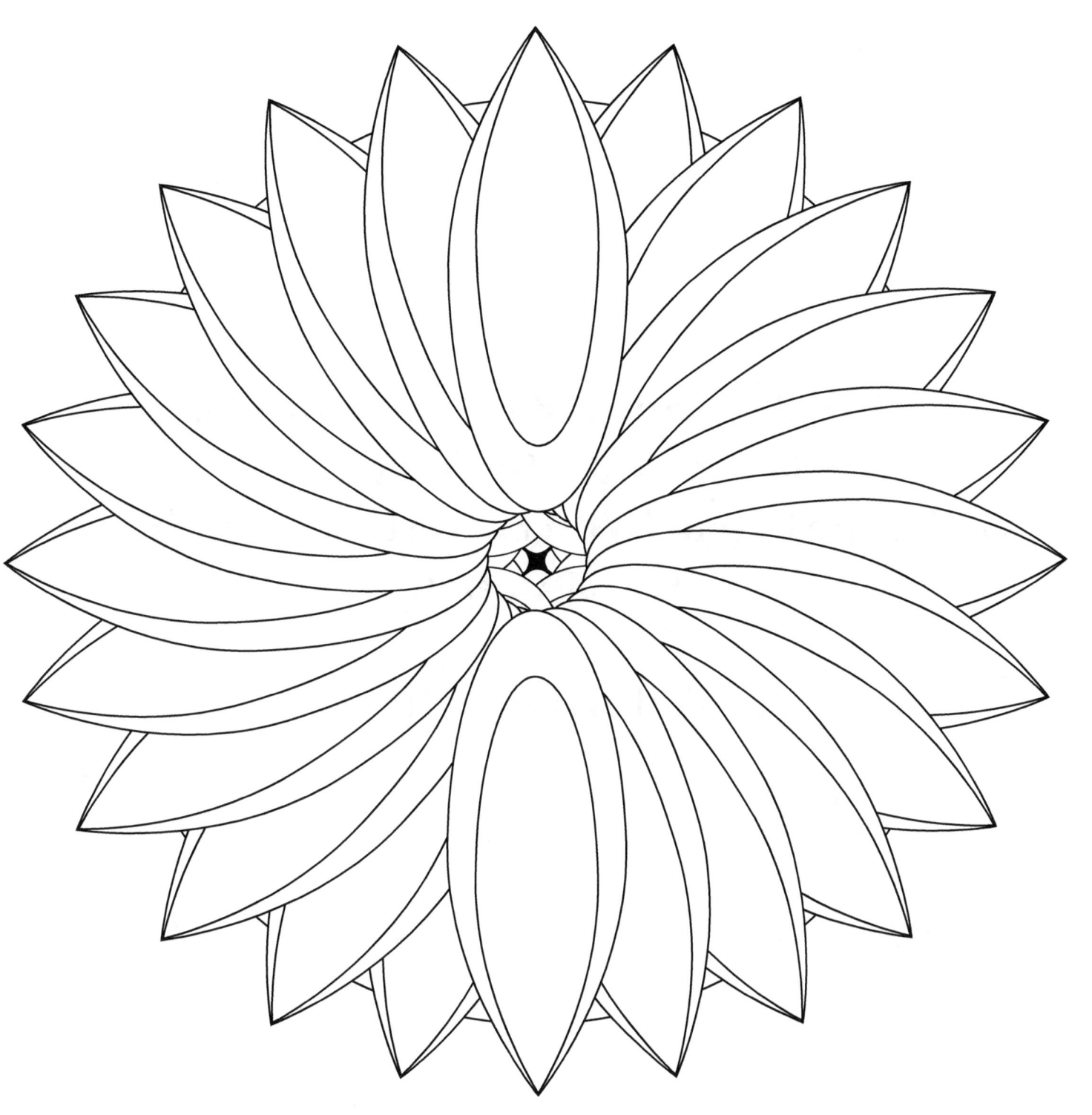

I hated every minute of training,
but I said, 'Don't quit.
Suffer now and live the rest of your life
as a champion.'

Muhammad Ali

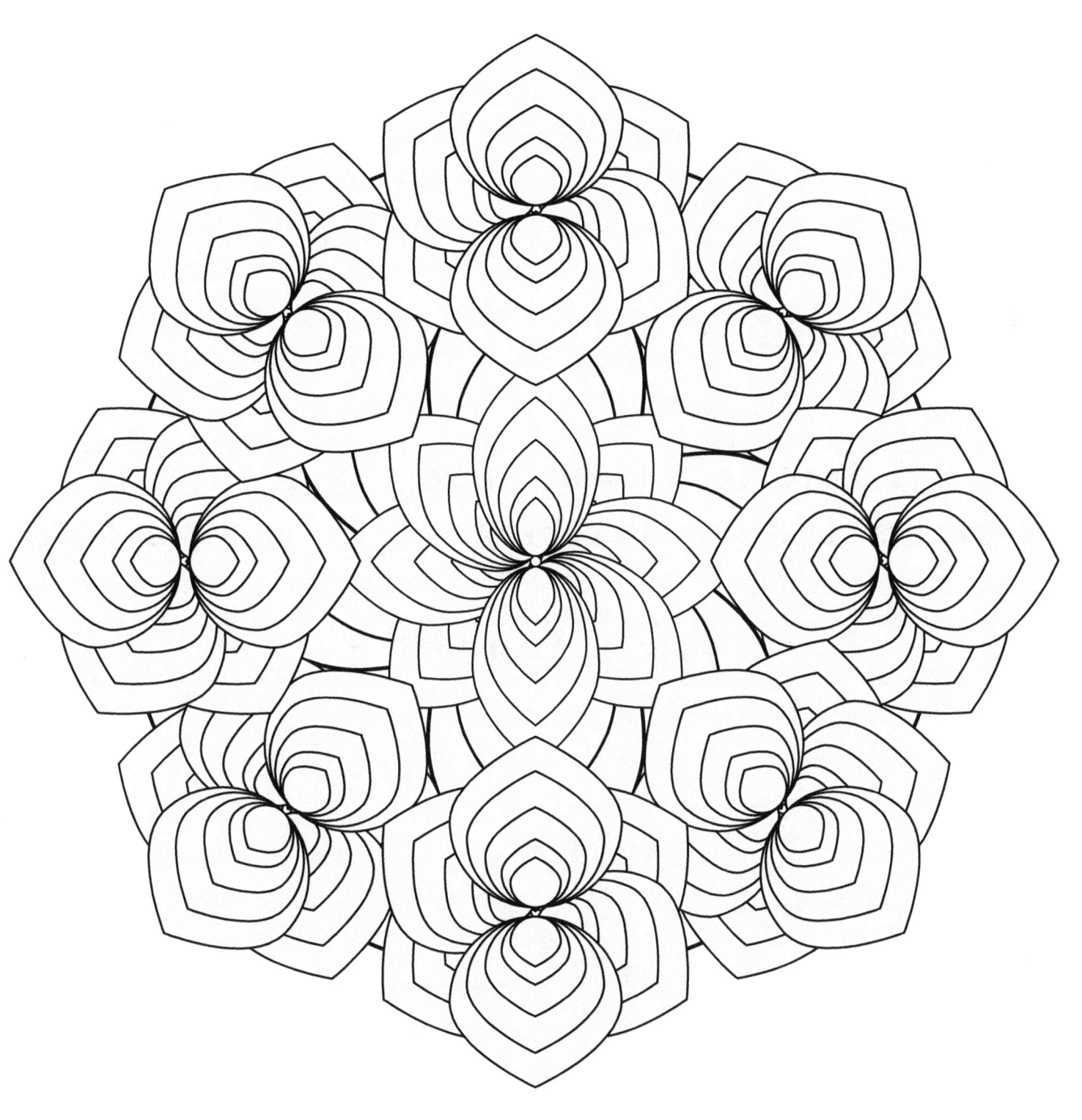

A hero is someone who has given
his or her life to something bigger than oneself.

Joseph Campbell

_____

_____

_____

_____

_____

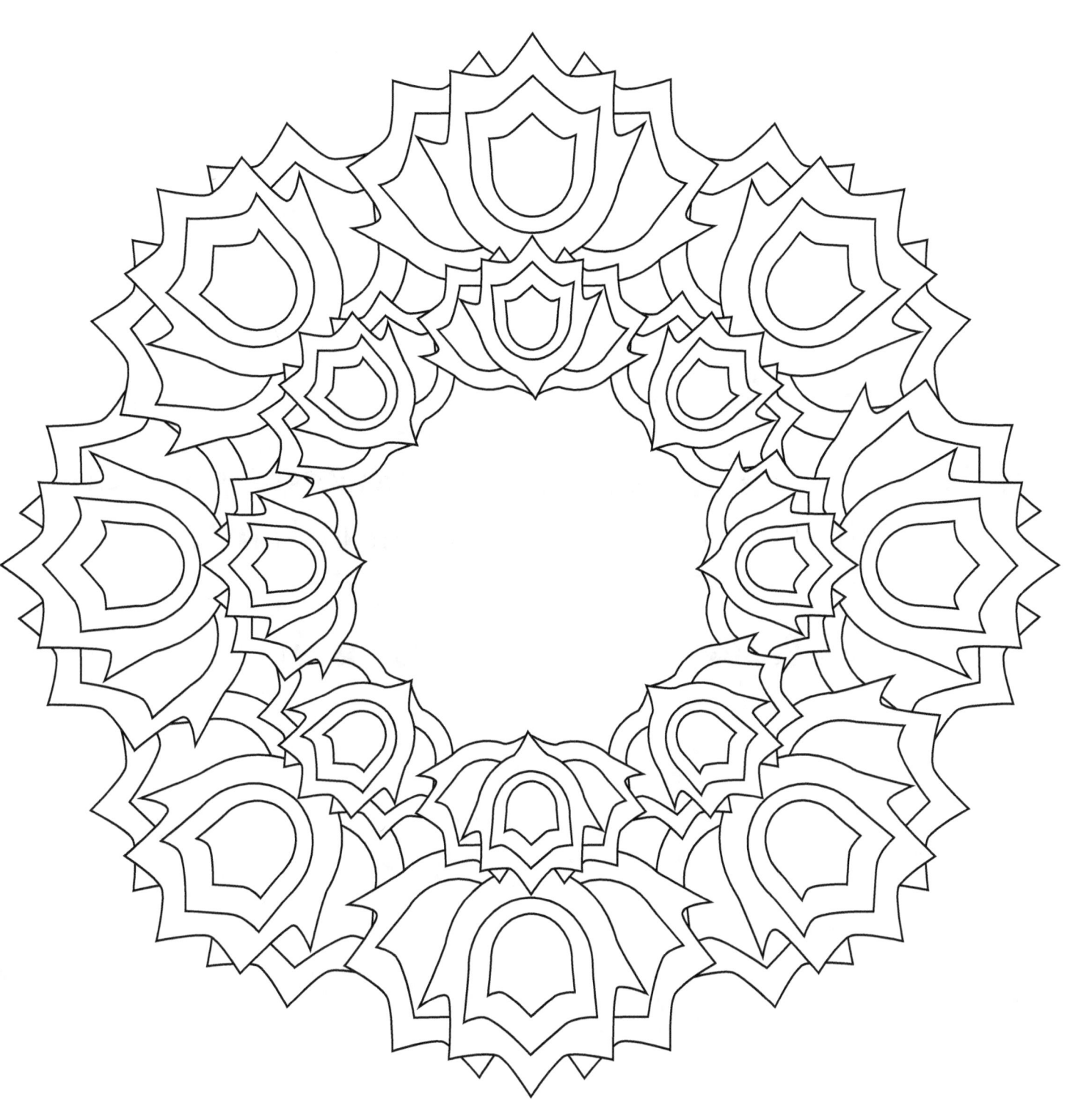

Don't judge each day by the harvest you reap
but by the seeds that you plant.

Robert Louis Stevenson

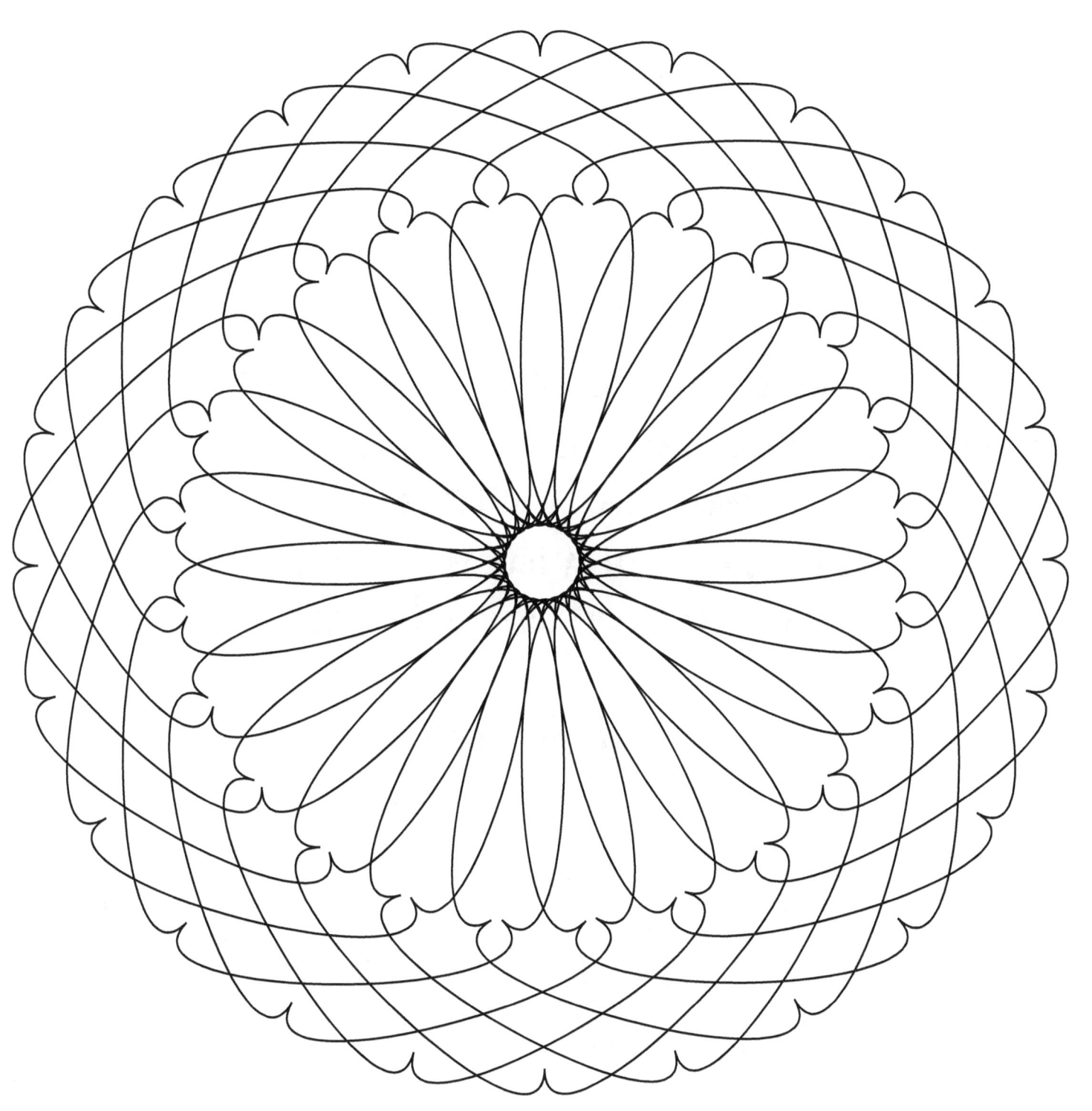

If you believe in yourself and
have dedication and pride - and never quit,
you'll be a winner.
The price of victory is high
but so are the rewards.

Paul Bryant

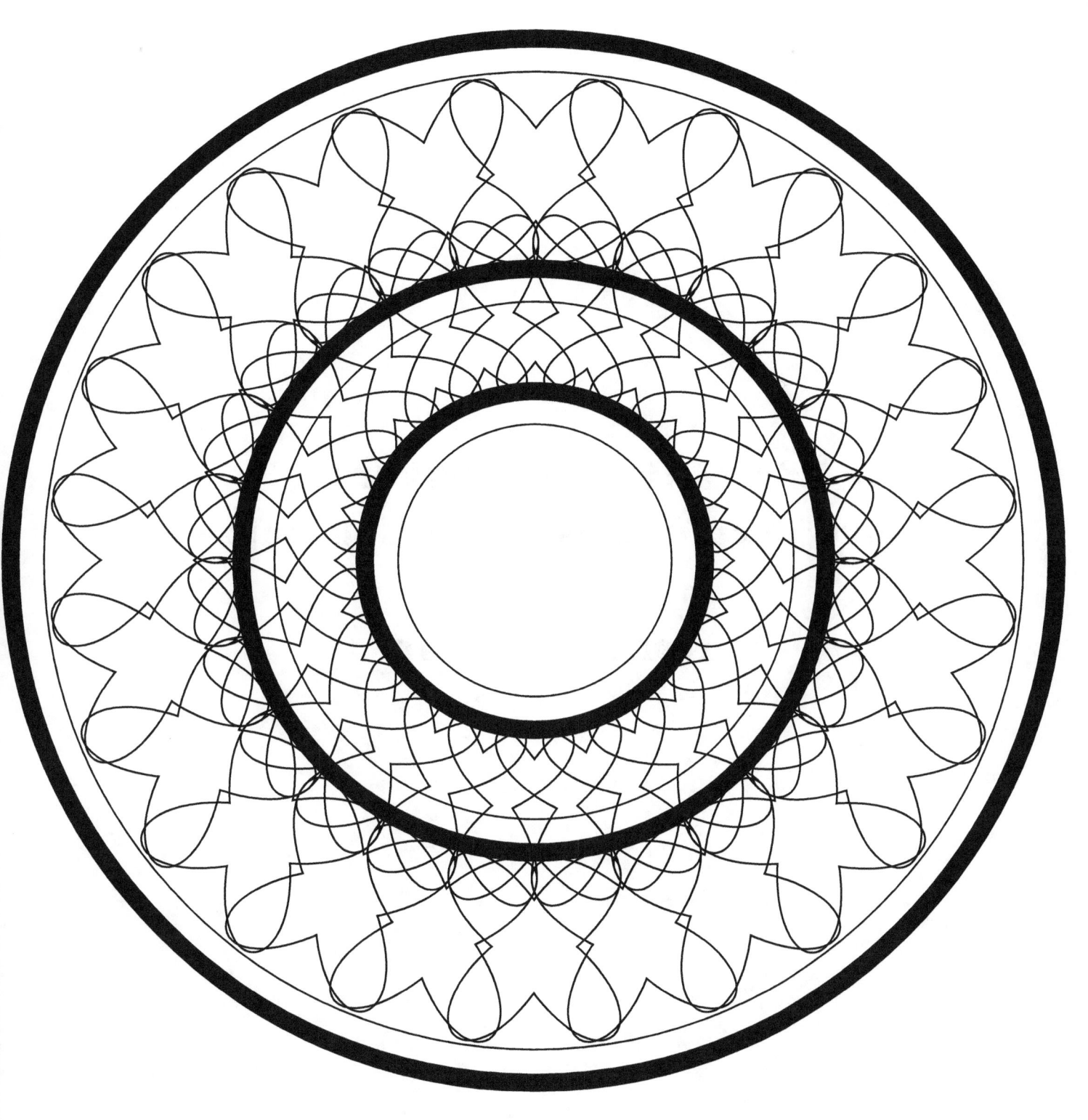

We can't help everyone,
but everyone can help someone.

Ronald Reagan

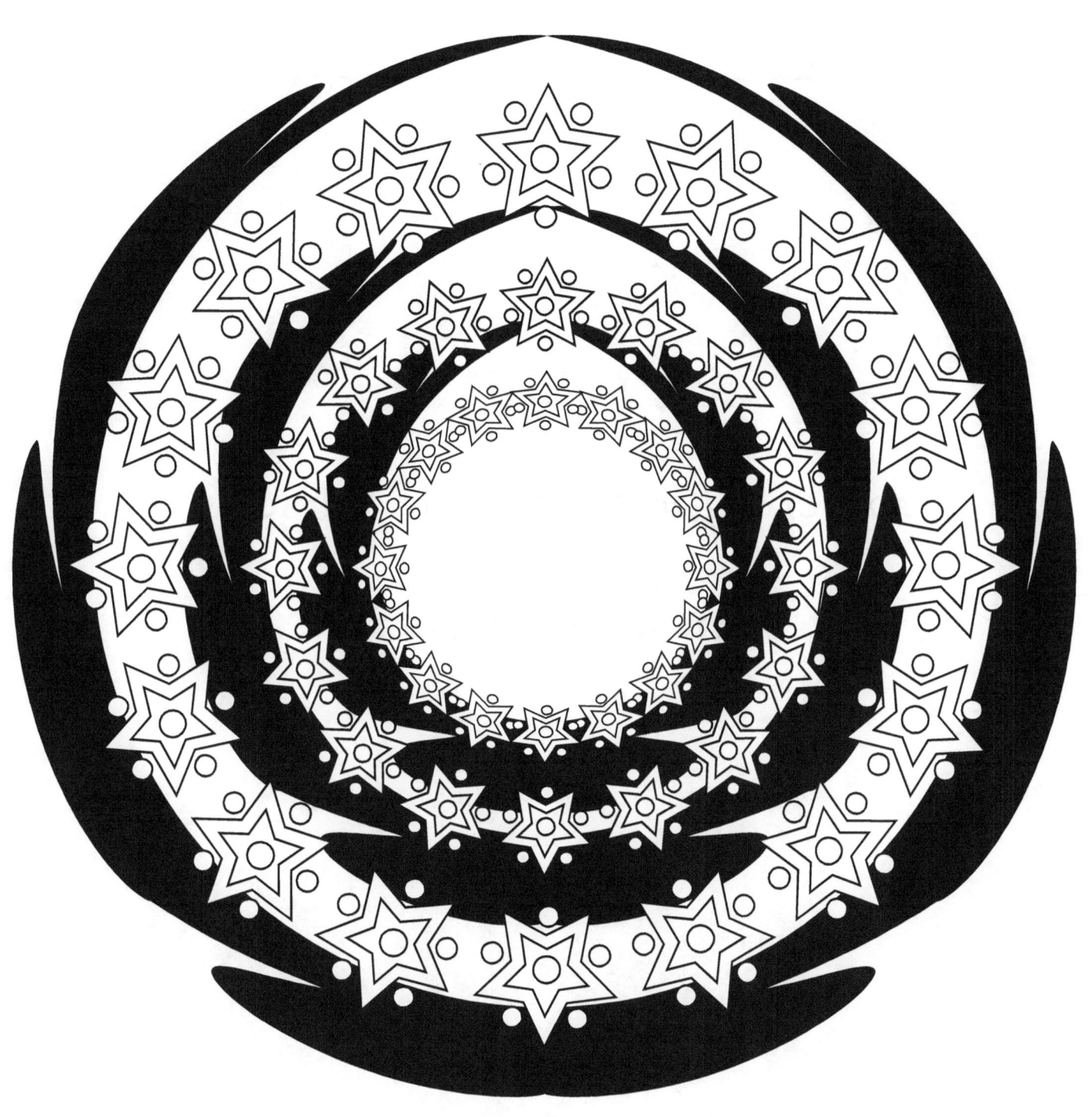

Out of difficulties grow miracles.

Jean de la Bruyère

_____

_____

_____

_____

_____

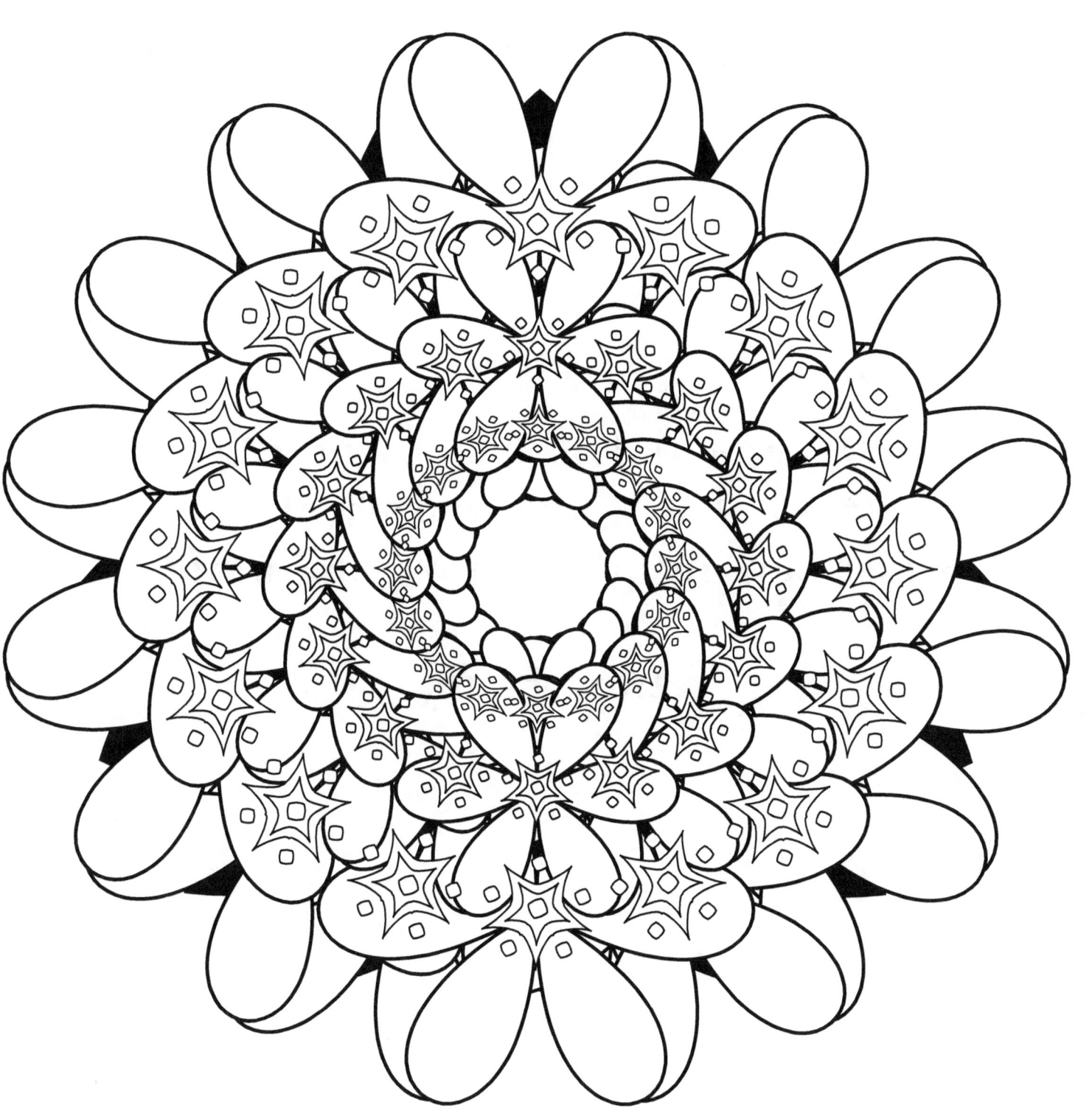

How wonderful it is that nobody
need wait a single moment
before starting to improve the world.

Anne Frank

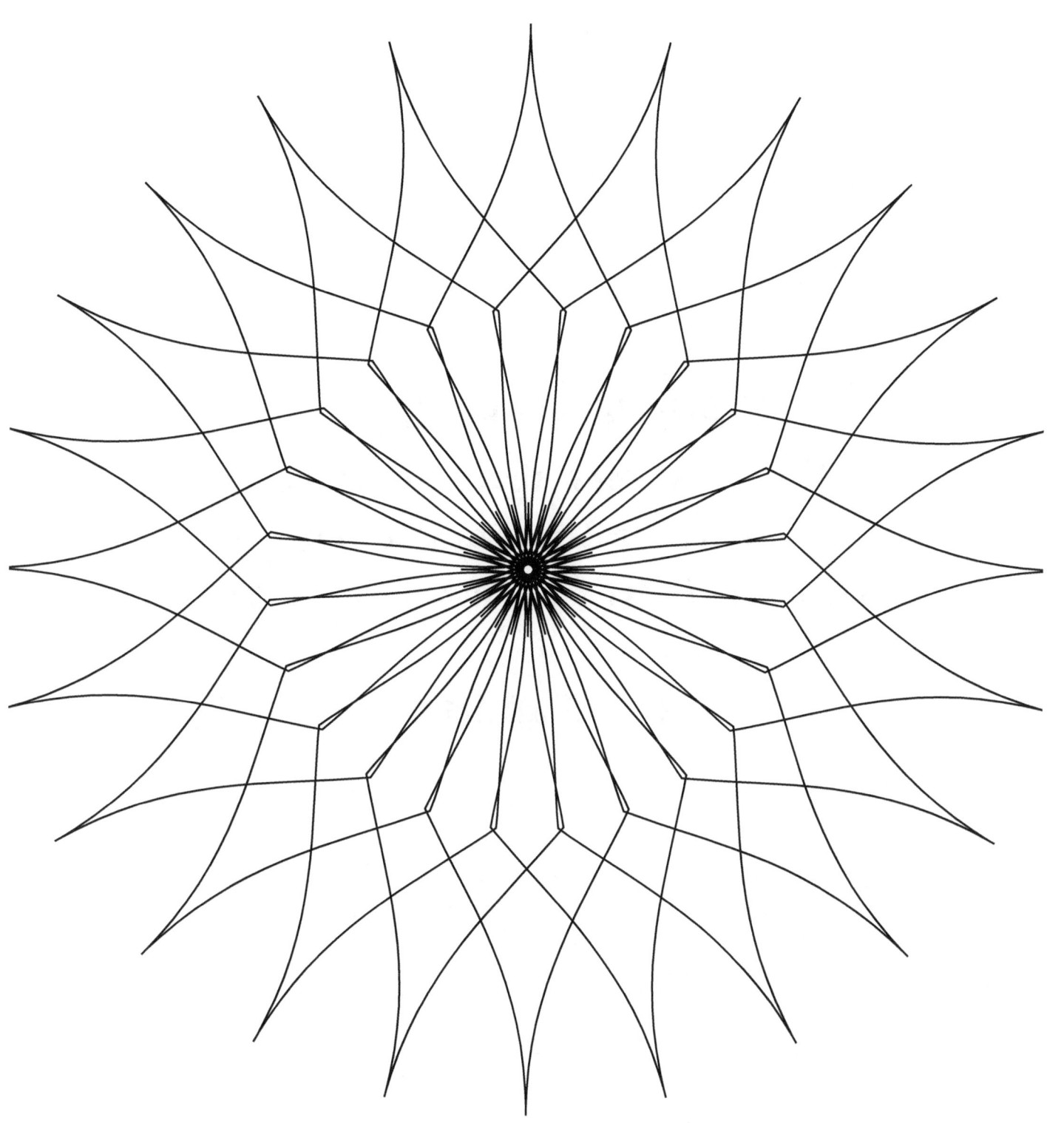

I will love the light
for it shows me the way,
yet I will endure the darkness
because it shows me the stars.

Og Mandino

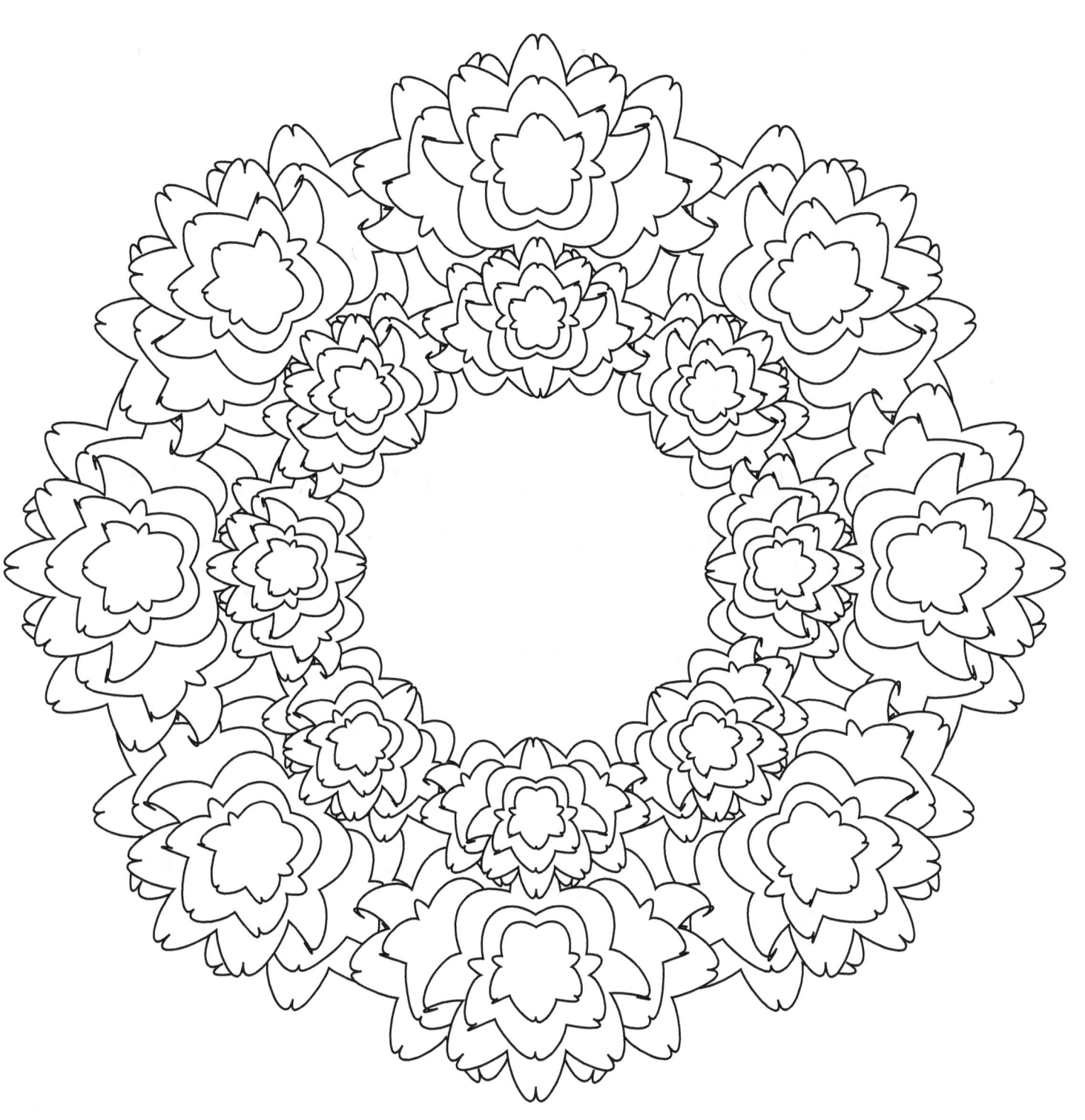

Keep your face always toward the sunshine
- and shadows will fall behind you.

Walt Whitman

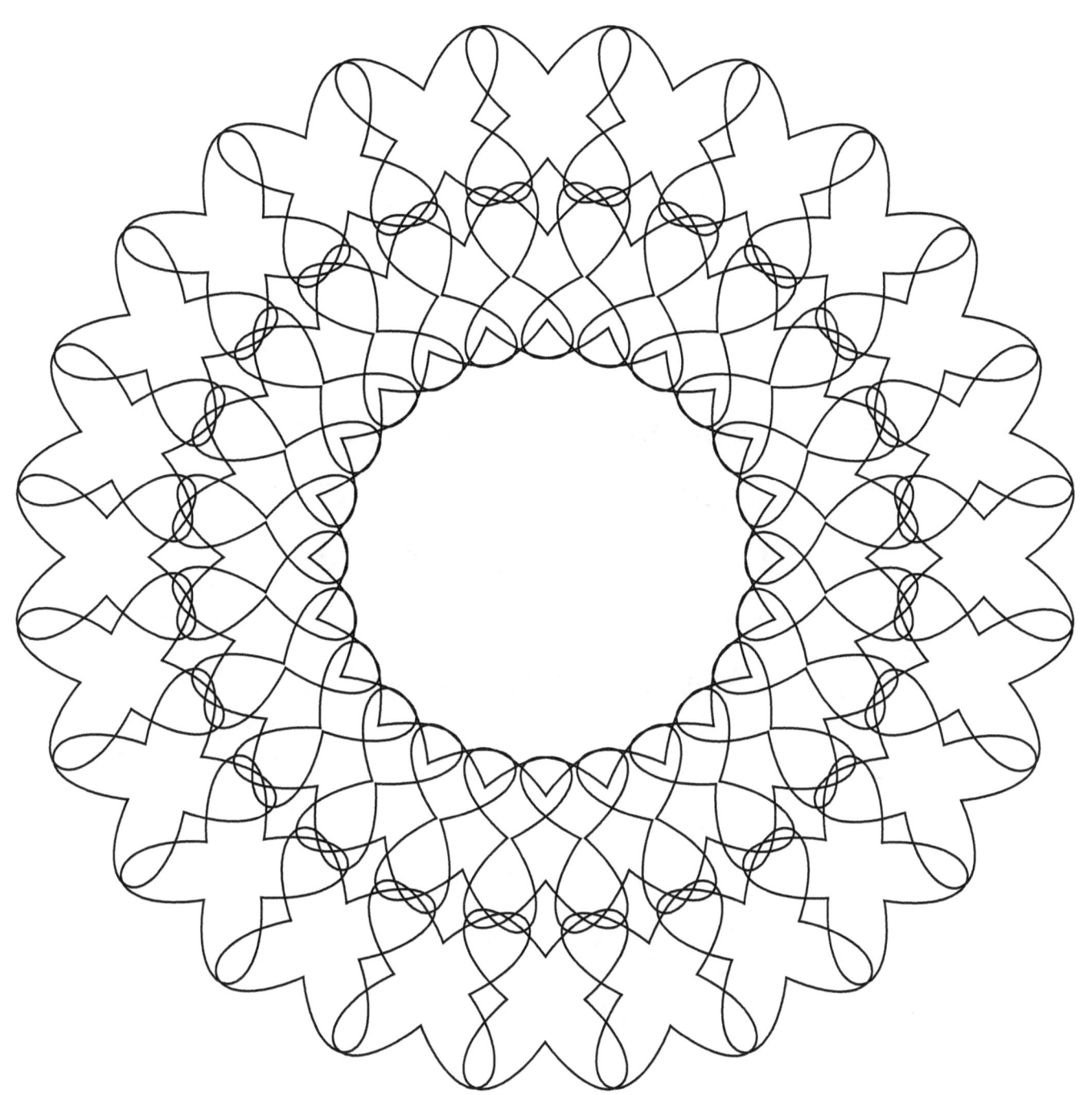

Let us remember: One book, one pen,
one child, and one teacher
can change the world.

Malala Yousafzai

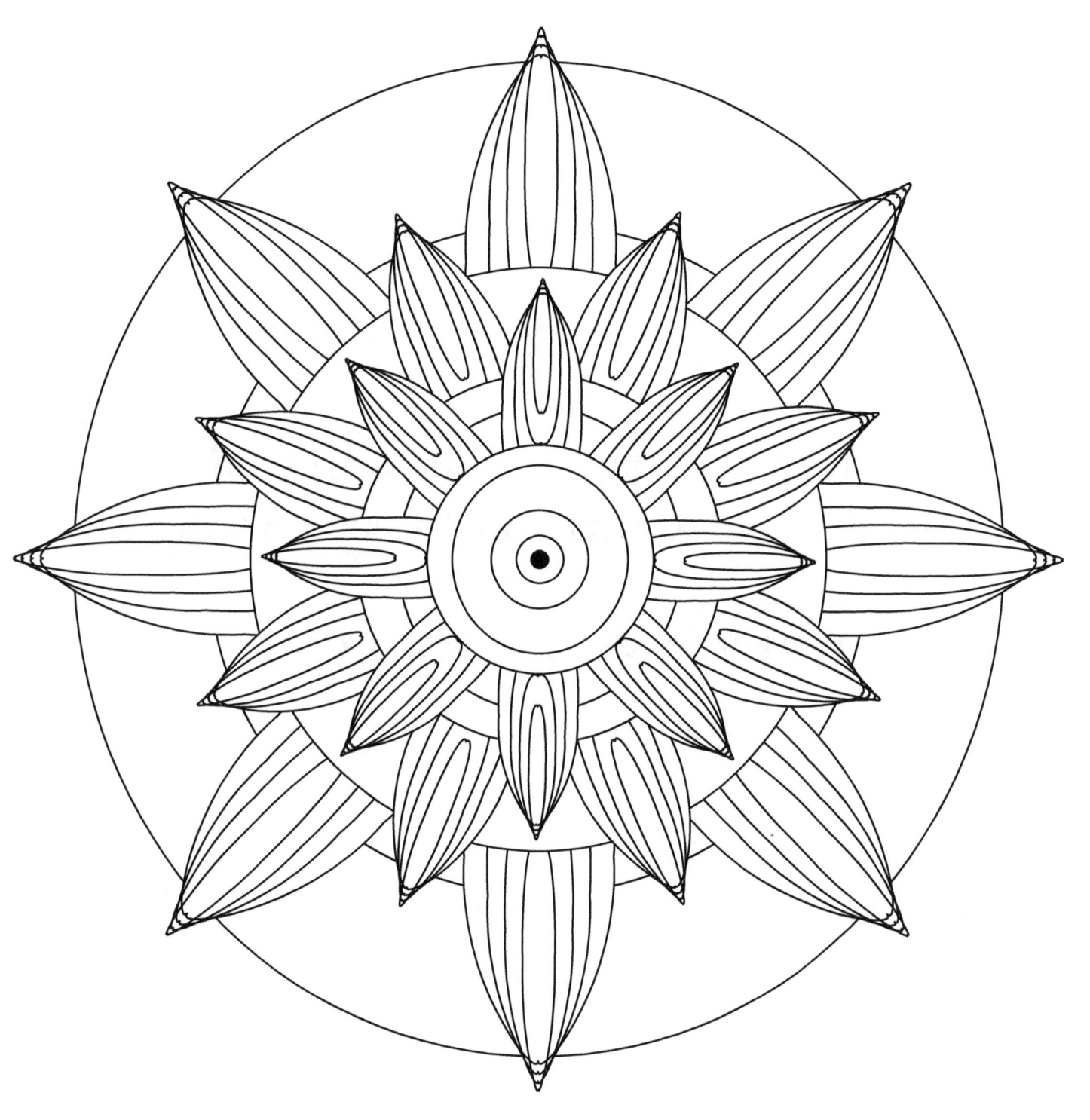

What makes the desert beautiful
is that somewhere it hides a well.

Antoine de Saint-Exupery

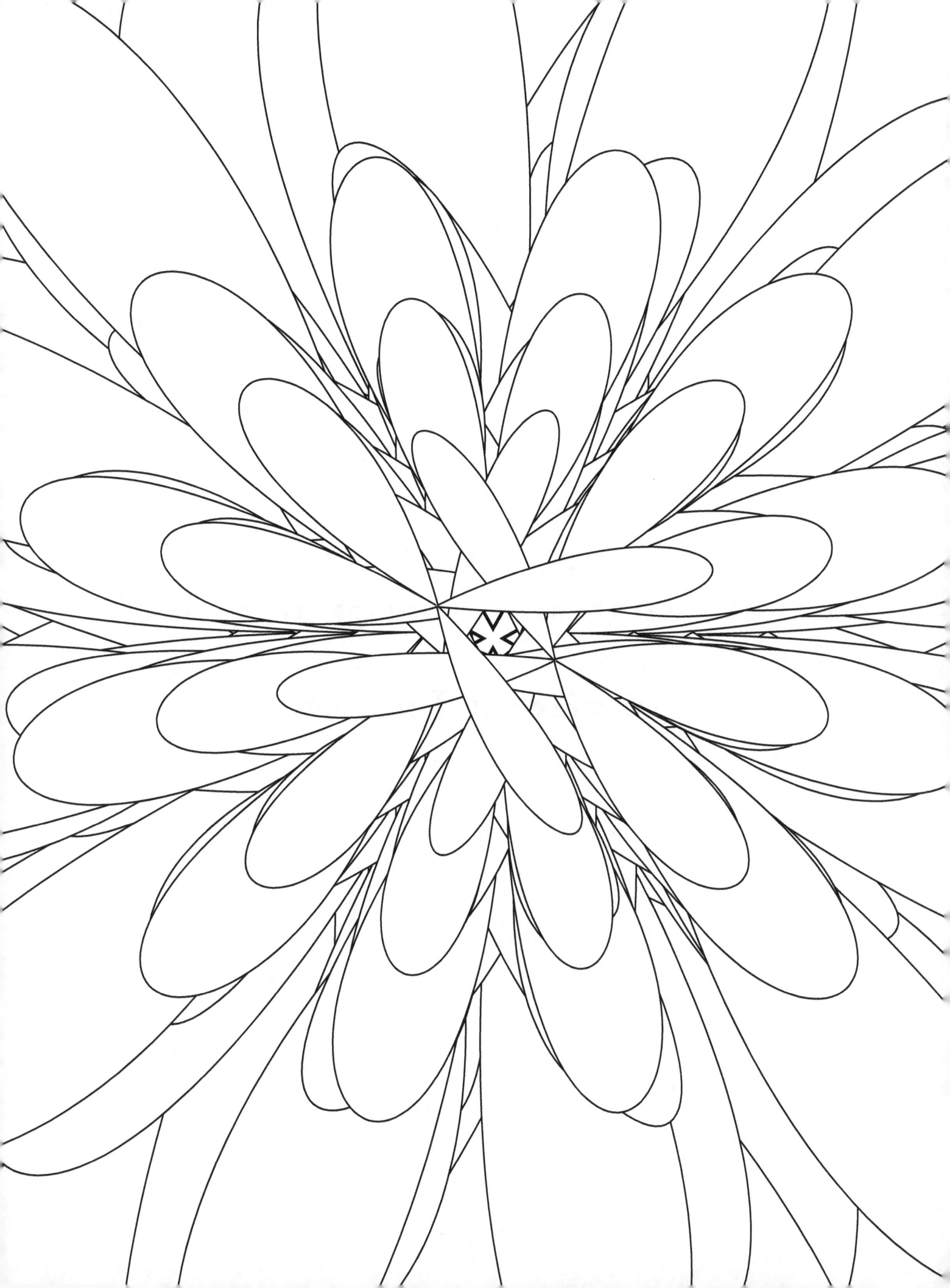

Give light,
and the darkness will disappear of itself.

Desiderius Erasmus

_____

_____

_____

_____

_____

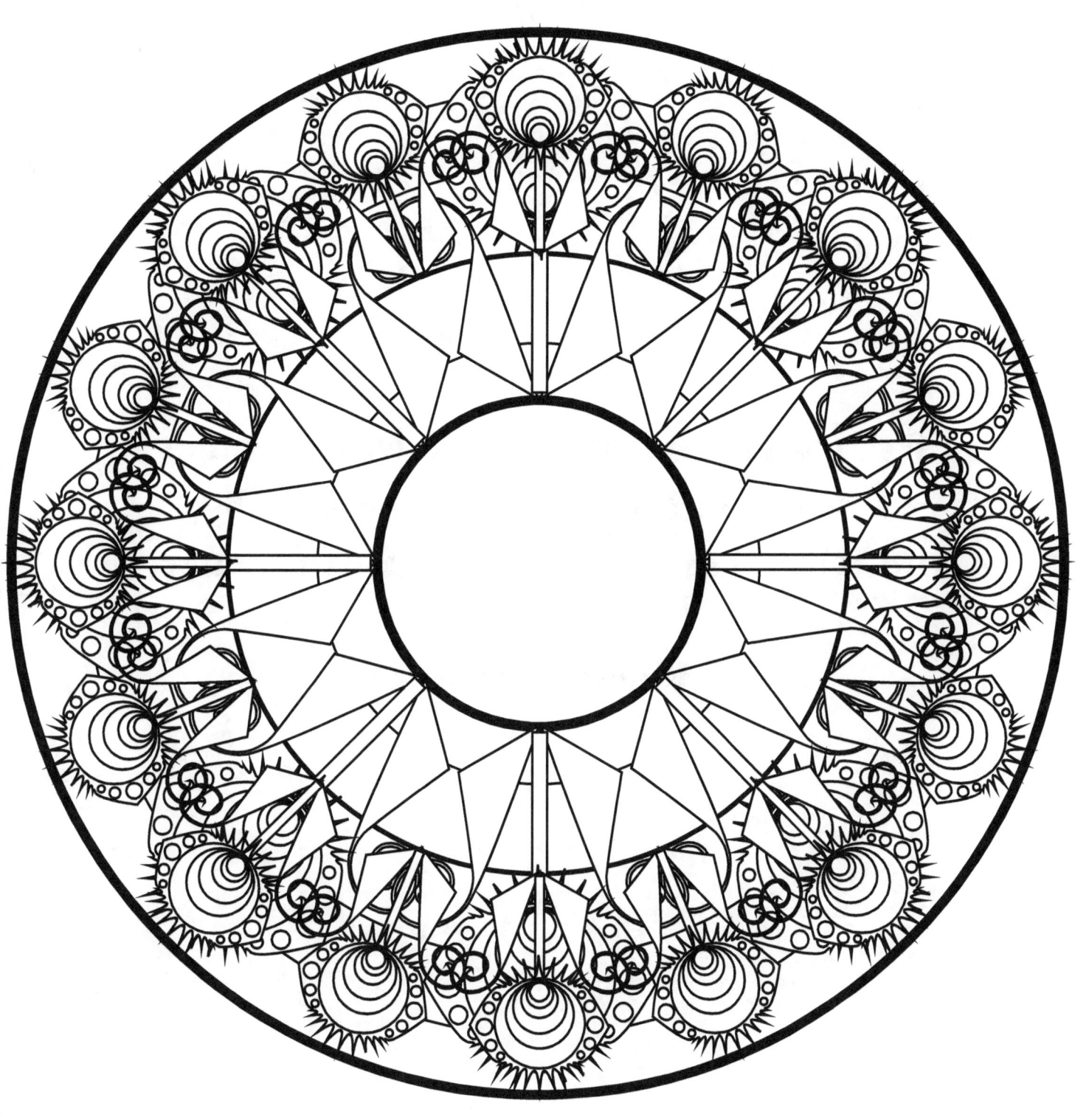

Two roads diverged in a wood and i
- i took the one less traveled by,
and that has made all the difference.

Robert Frost

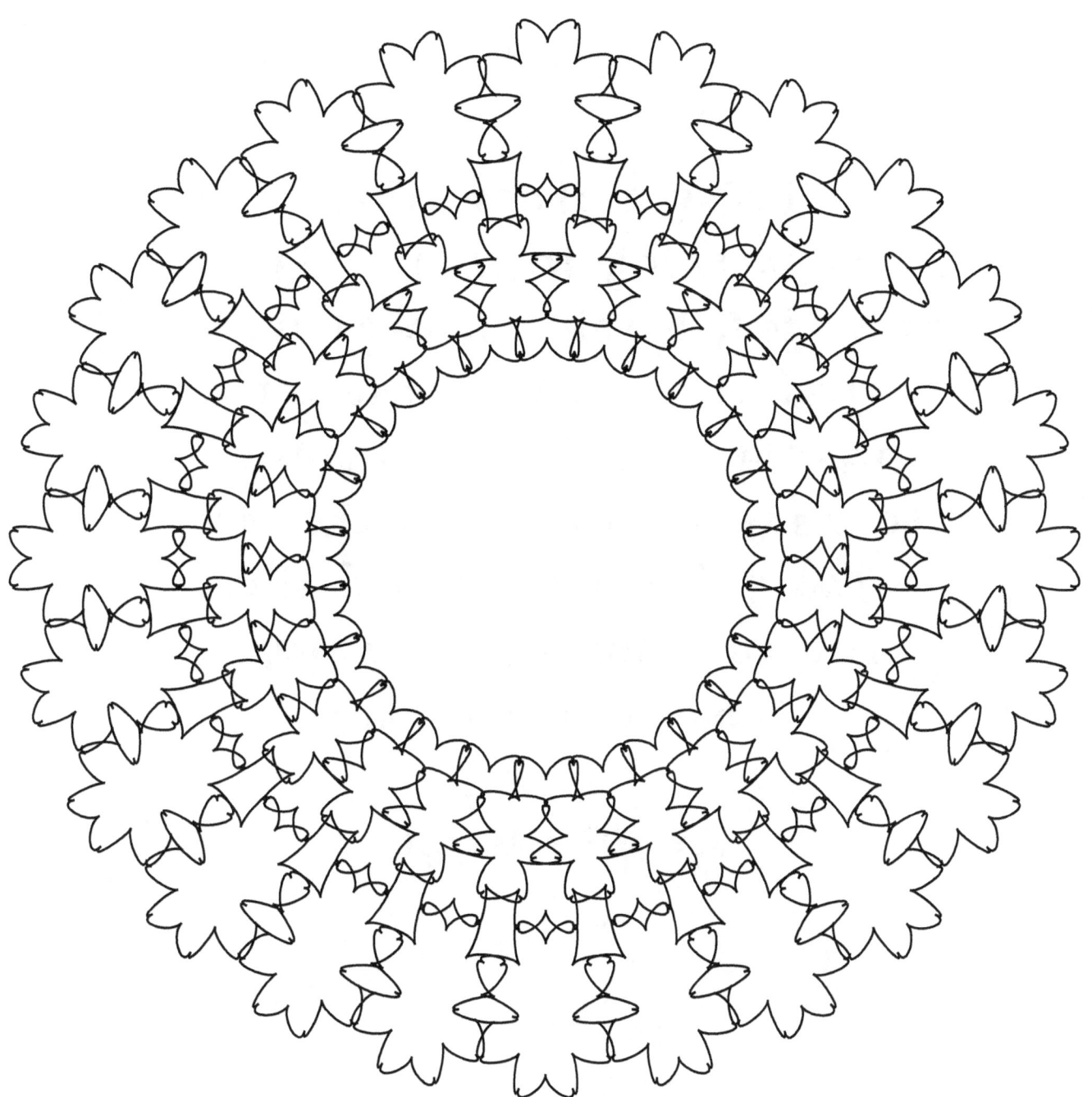

Today i choose life.
Every morning when i wake up
i can choose joy, happiness, negativity, pain...
To feel the freedom that comes
from being able to continue
to make mistakes and choices
- today i choose to feel life,
not to deny my humanity
but embrace it.

Kevyn Aucoin

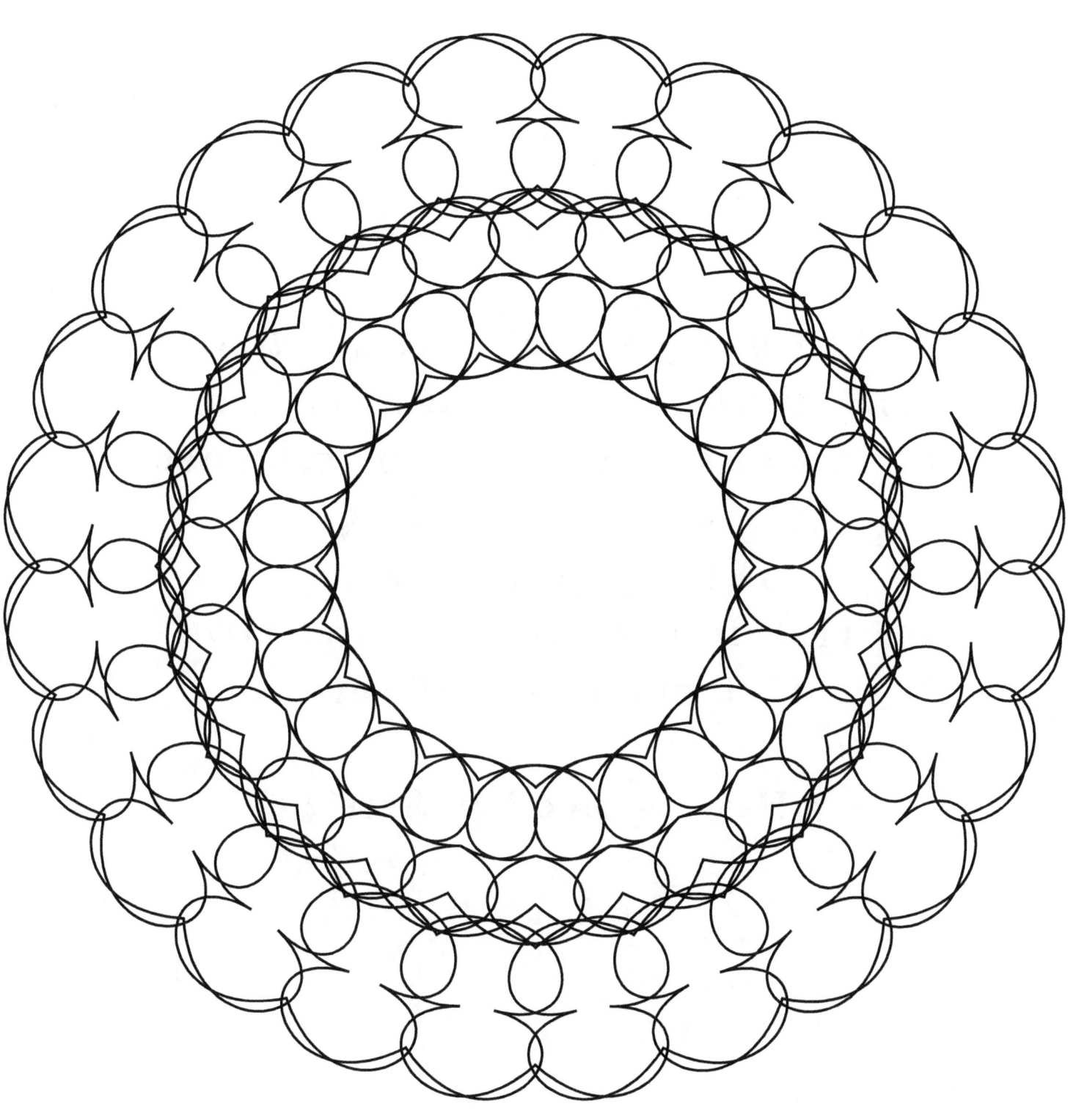

When you get into a tight place
and everything goes against you,
till it seems as though you could not
hang on a minute longer,
never give up then,
for that is just the place and time
that the tide will turn.

Harriet Beecher Stowe

_____

_____

_____

_____

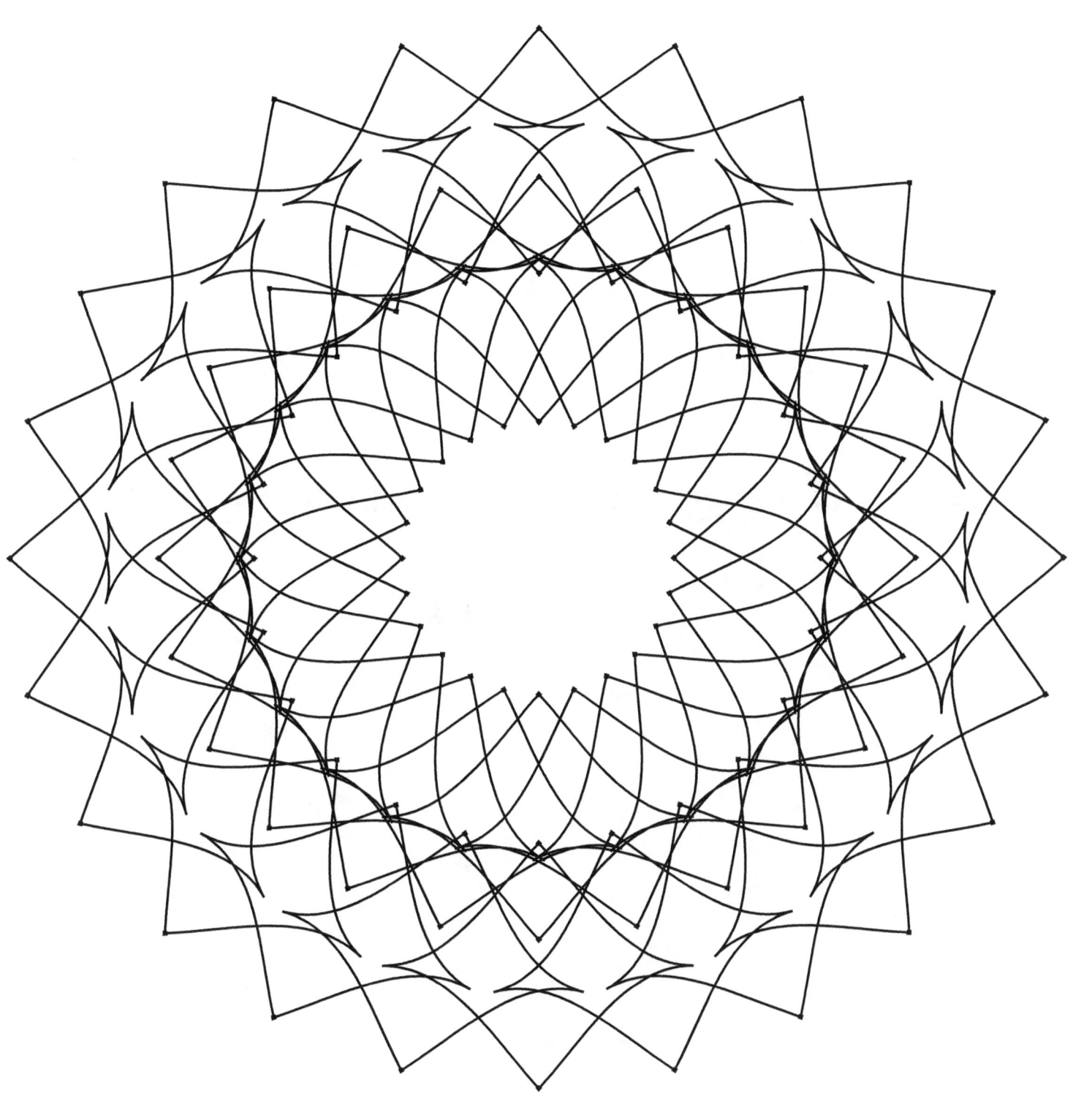

Whoever is happy will make others happy too.

Anne Frank

_____

_____

_____

_____

_____

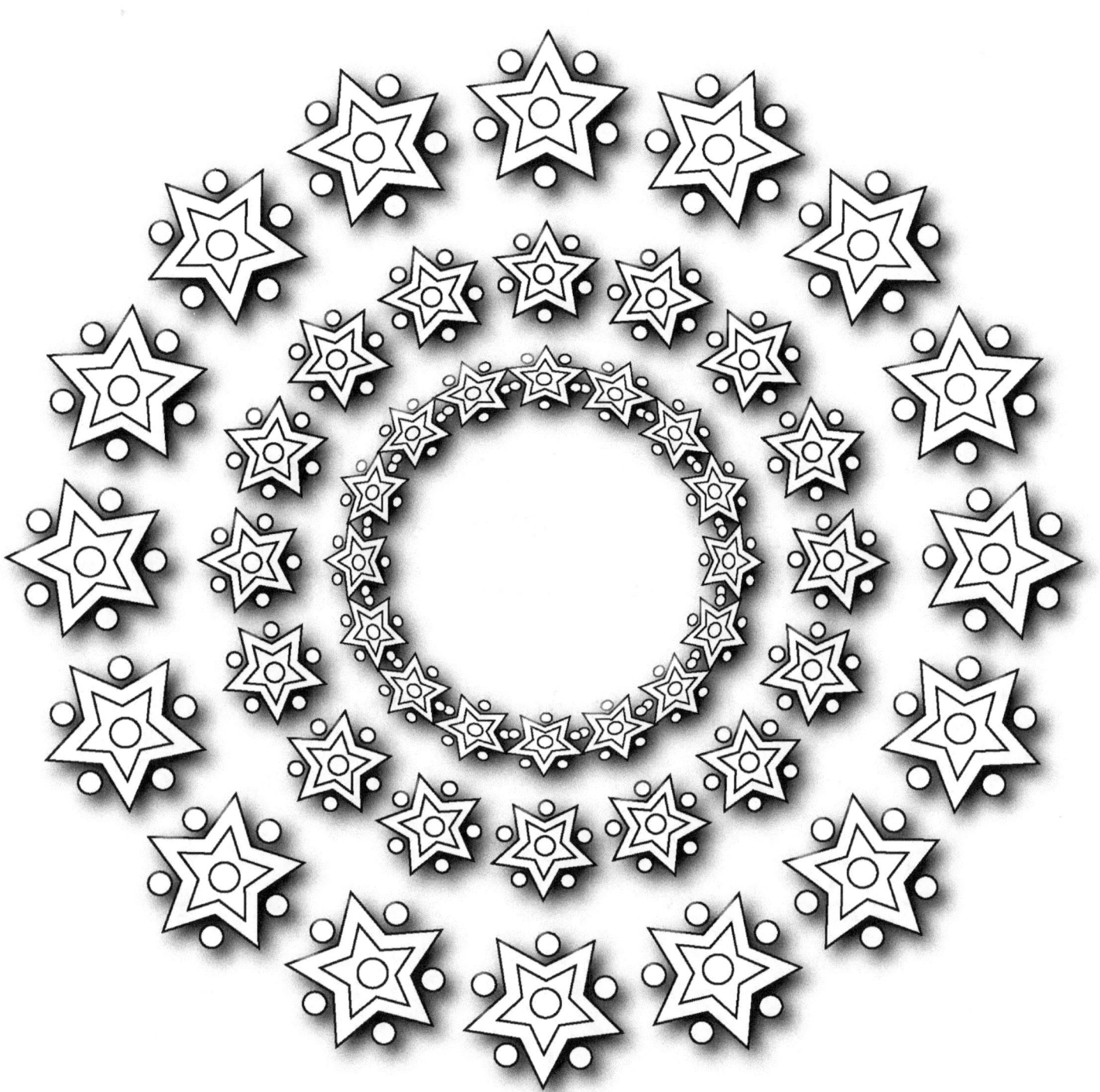

What lies behind you
and what lies in front of you,
pales in comparison
to what lies inside of you.

Ralph Waldo Emerson

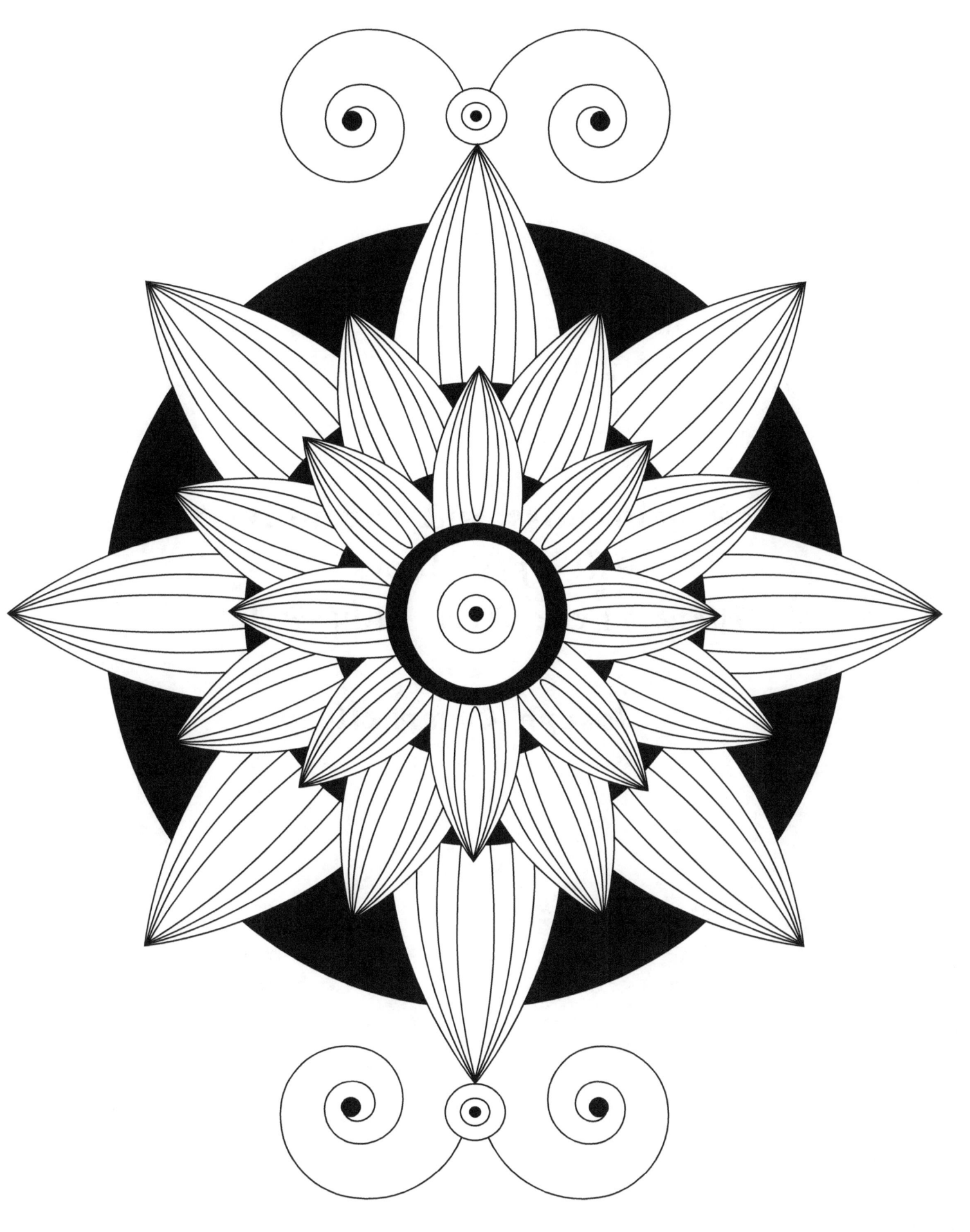

Follow your bliss and the universe
will open doors
where there were only walls.

Joseph Campbell

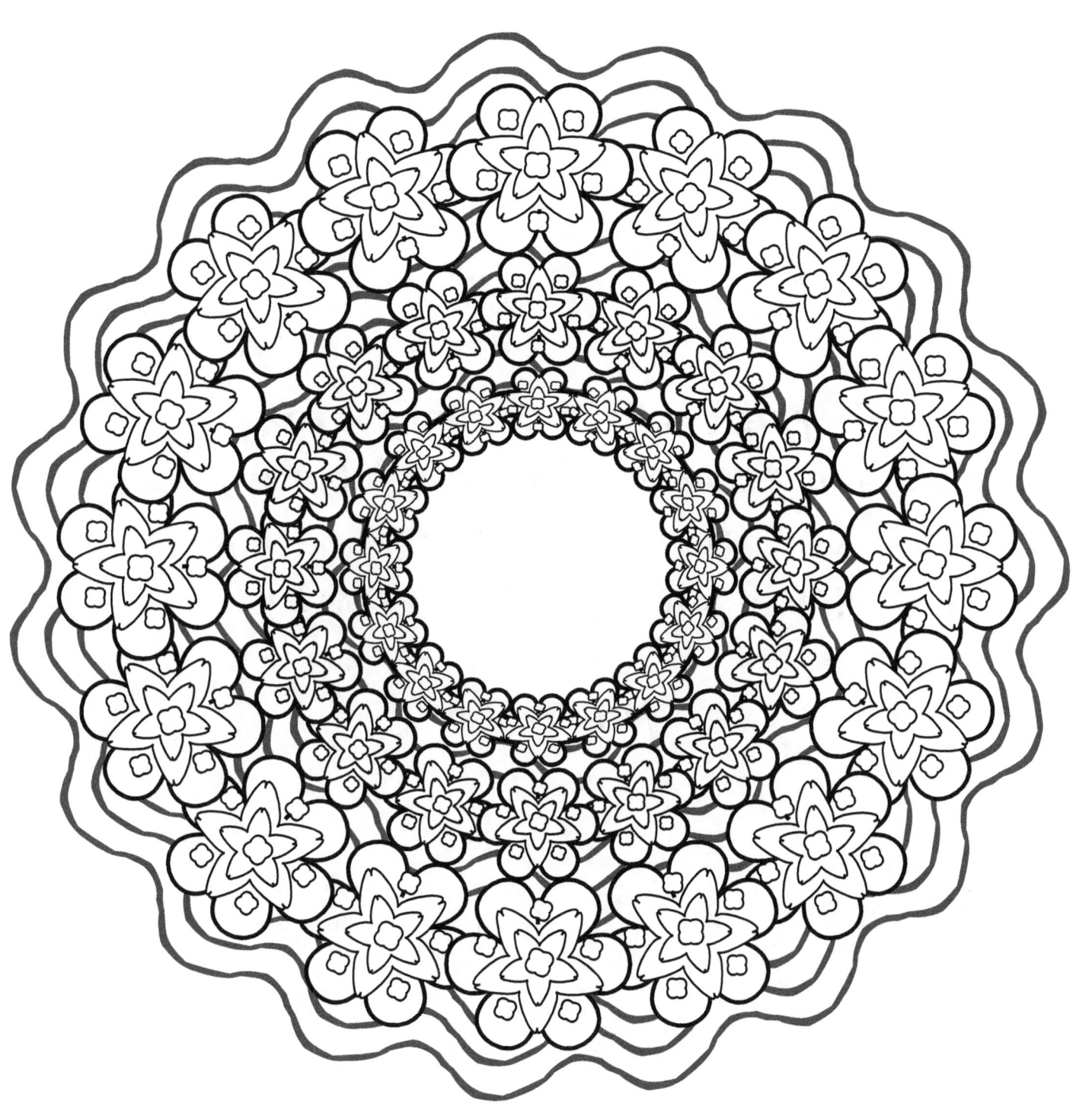

Happiness is not something
you postpone for the future;
it is something
you design for the present.

Jim Rohn

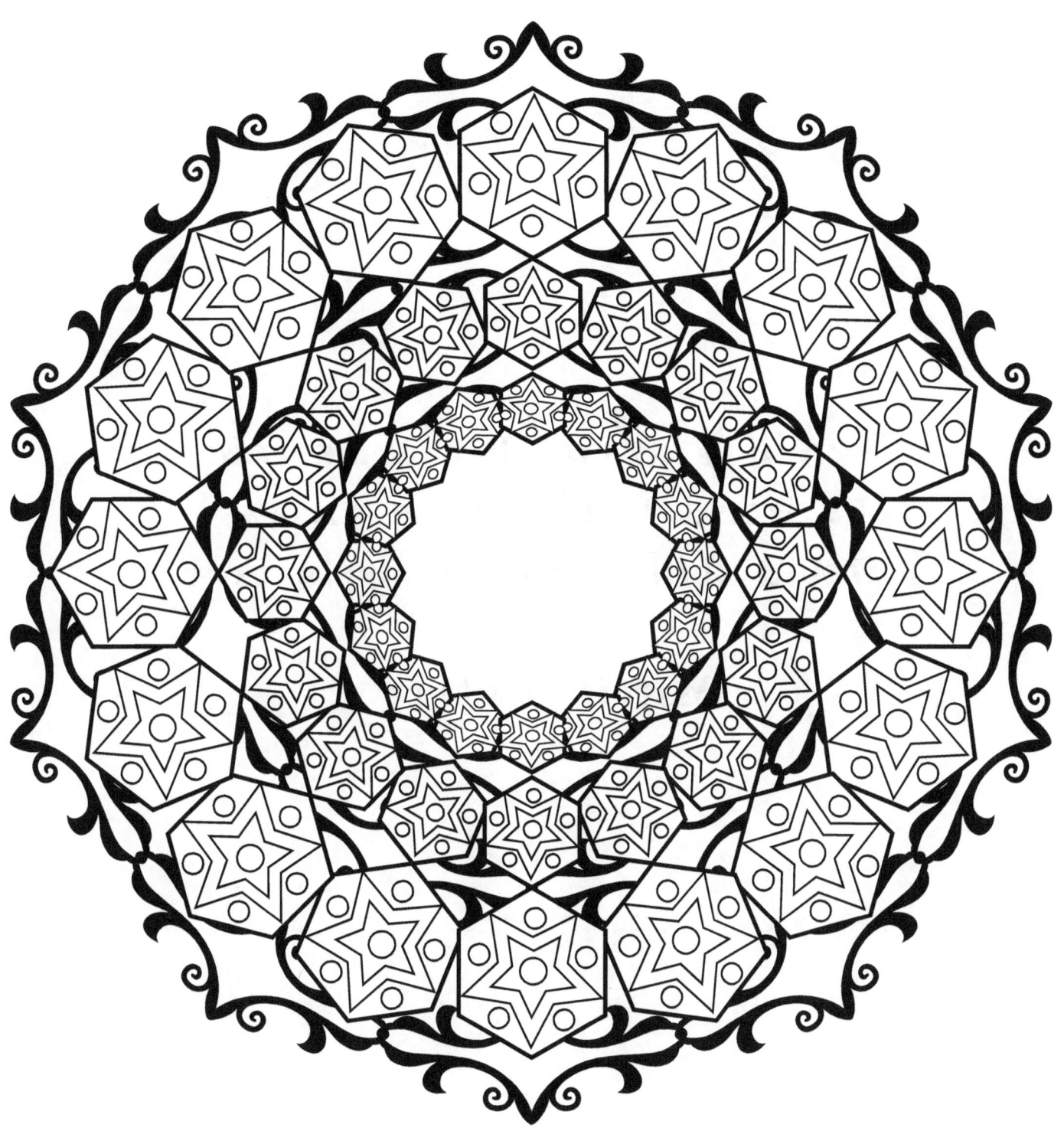

Even if I knew that tomorrow
the world would go to pieces,
I would still plant my apple tree.

Martin Luther

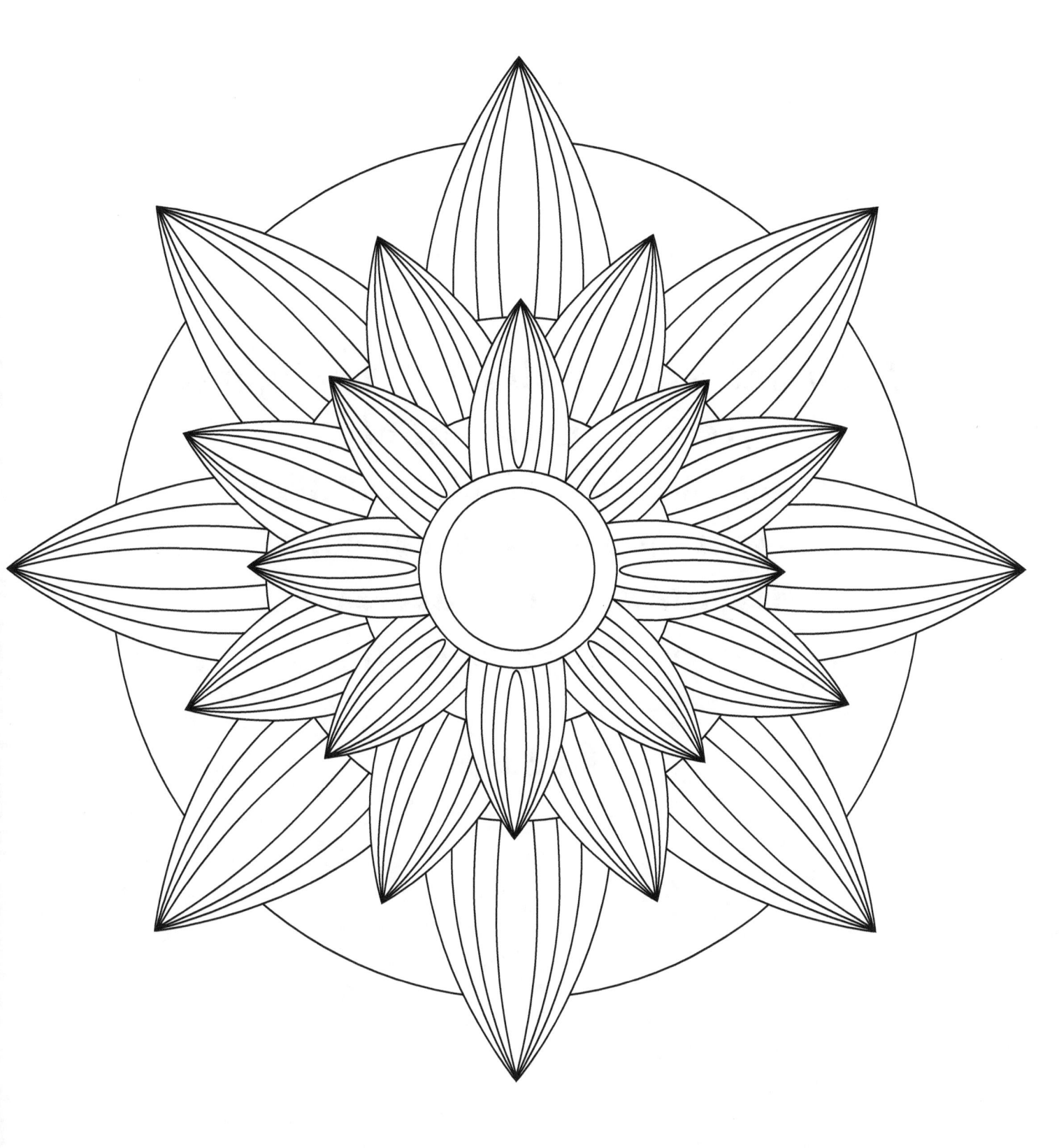

Thousands of candles can be lighted
from a single candle,
and the life of the candle
will not be shortened.
Happiness never decreases
by being shared.

Buddha

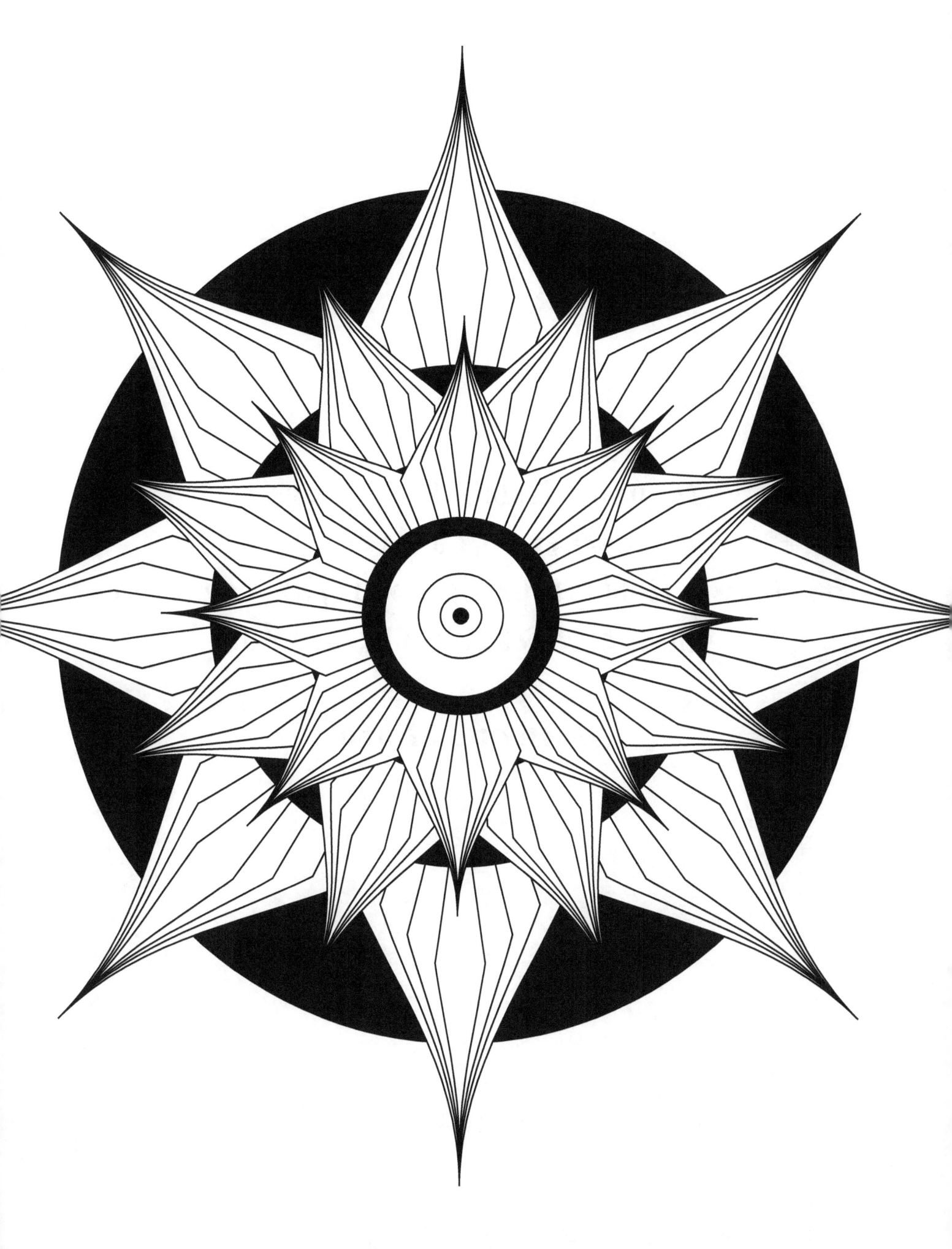

Do your little bit of good
where you are;
its those little bits of good put together
that overwhelm the world.

Desmond Tutu